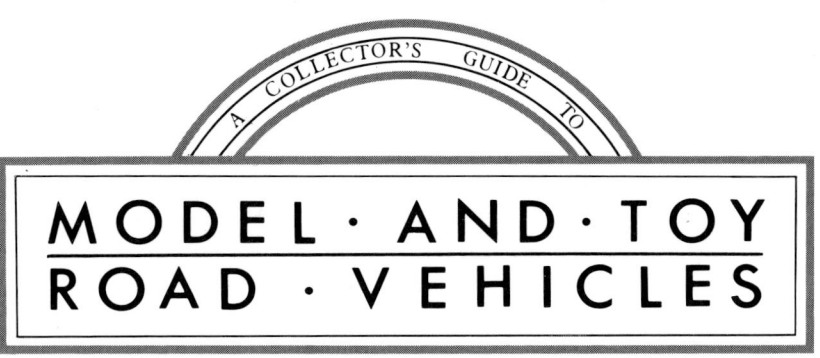

MODEL · AND · TOY
ROAD · VEHICLES

MICHAEL WORTHINGTON-WILLIAMS
AND
PETER ROBERTS

LONGMAN
LONDON AND NEW YORK

Longman Group Limited
Longman House, Burnt Mill, Harlow
Essex CM20 2JE, England
Associated companies throughout the world

*Published in the United States of America
by Longman Inc., New York*

First published 1985

British Library Cataloguing in Publication Data
Worthington-Williams, Michael
A collector's guide to model and toy road vehicles.
1. Automobiles – Models – Collectors and collecting.
I. Title   II. Roberts, Peter, 1925–
629.2′2122   TL237

ISBN 0-582-40612-9

Library of Congress Cataloging in Publication Data
Worthington-Williams, Michael.
A collector's guide to model and toy road vehicles.

Bibliography: p.
Includes index.
1. Automobiles – Models – Collectors and collecting.
I. Roberts, Peter, 1925–   II. Title.
TL237.W67   1984   629.2′21   83-7976

ISBN 0-582-40612-9

Set in 10/12 pt Plantin.
Produced by Longman Group (FE) Ltd
Printed in Hong Kong

Dedicated to William Boddy
and the late W. H. Charnock, enthusiasts
(in the widest sense) and visionaries, both.

CONTENTS

PREFACE

It has been said that the growth of interest in things past and, indeed, the growth of nostalgia itself, has been very largely a reaction to the rapid changes wrought by the advanced technology that has its roots in the industrial revolution of the late eighteenth century.

It is ironic, therefore, that the subject-matter of this book – which most will admit is capable of stirring the strongest possible feelings of nostalgia – would probably never have existed had not that same industrial revolution provided both the technology and the demand.

The invention of machine production tin plate – thin sheet steel plated with tin – dictated early in the nineteenth century the form which the tin toy would follow, with little basic change, for the next one hundred and fifty years; the die-cast toy which superseded it is very much a child of the twentieth century.

This is not to say, of course, that toys did not exist previously. Archaeologists have ample proof that toys played as important a part in the lives of children in ancient Rome or Pompeii as they do today, and who is to say that Stone-Age boys and girls did not fashion for themselves some miniature edition of father's crude implements?

Until the advent of the industrial revolution, however, toymaking remained little more than a cottage industry at most, and, in the very early days even in and around Nuremberg, much of the work was done by outworkers in their own homes. More of Nuremberg later, but what the revolution provided was the technology for large-scale toy manufacture – mass production, in fact – the necessary tin plate, the factories, and a large pool of skilled labour.

It also helped to create the new monied middle class who could afford both playtime and playthings, and to a lesser extent created a demand for cheaper products from its own workforce, just as Henry Ford created a demand for Model 'T's by paying his own workers sufficient wages to enable them to afford one.

As the technology of the industrial revolution progressed, so man's achievements were mirrored in miniature in the toys which the factories produced. The nineteenth and early twentieth centuries were the ages of steam and the railways; thus we find a predominance of trains among the early toys.

The popularisation of the motor car in Britain was slow. Restrictive legislation and a horse-oriented hierarchy stifled its early development. As a result, toy motor cars were also slow to catch on. It was not until the Edwardian era, when the car itself gained general acceptance, that model and toy versions proliferated.

But although they might echo the full-size locomotives, trams, omnibuses – and later cars and aeroplanes – of the grown-up world, the early tin toys still retained an element of folk art inherited from the early 'cottage industry' days. Their simplification, crudity and elements of fantasy gave just that combination of ingredients likely to appeal to the imagination of a child; herein lies the magic of their appeal to adult collectors.

As Cecil Gibson, writing the introduction to his *History of British Dinky Toys* in 1964, so candidly puts it, one of his motives for writing the book was the 'pure nostalgia for childhood's toys when I looked through the old Meccano and Hornby catalogues, a nostalgia for that lost world of the thirties . . .'.

So yes, we are concerned with nostalgia. Nostalgia on a personal level, as when we discover in some dusty corner a once-favourite model from our own childhood bringing back nursery memories, and nostalgia on a general level when viewing with interest and amusement examples of the toys played with by our parents' generation, and that of our grandparents.

But there is more to the collecting of toys than this. There is, as David Pressland (one of today's most distinguished collectors) says, the discovery of the art of the toy – the art of their design, their creation and execution – which is generally only capable of appreciation in adulthood. Thus we have the best of both worlds – a genuine re-creation of the joy of our childhood plus an added bonus of insight, which only the passing years have been capable of bestowing.

As any experienced collector will tell you, the study of the history of toys in general is, as yet, an inexact science. The study of early toy vehicles is no exception and documentary evidence is, sadly, scant at best and in many cases totally lacking.

This is only to be expected at this stage of development of toy collecting. After all, it is only in recent years that the history of full-sized vehicles has been considered worthy of scholarship. The encouraging thing is that, as time passes, the sum of published knowledge increases rather than decreases.

A growing awareness of the need to preserve not only the toys themselves, but also their makers' catalogues and literature, the original boxes in which they came, contemporary journals, advertisements and all connected ephemera, will help us to build up a more complete picture, but there will always be mysteries.

Many of the early toymakers eschewed both catalogues and trademarks, marketed their products through wholesalers or under other makers' names and generally made life difficult for present-day toy historians. No matter. Together with the established houses they have left for us (and are continuing to leave) a rich legacy in no way diminished by anonymity.

In this book we will introduce you to a representative selection of both the famous and the obscure, for it would be quite impossible to cover all the known makes and models of vehicle in a book with even ten times the number of pages available – or even in ten similar-sized volumes. If we have conveyed, in some small measure, however, the fascination and the nostalgia generated by these art works in miniature – the beautiful and the bizarre, the primitive and the sophisticated – then we shall not have failed in our object.

Capel Iwan 1984

ACKNOWLEDGEMENTS

Many people have assisted in the preparation of this book, and to them all the authors extend their grateful thanks. In particular, however, they would like to mention the following for photographic facilities, for the loan of photographs and the benefit of advice freely given:

Jon Baddeley
Phillipe Charbonneaux
David Filsell
Musée de l'Automobiles Françaises, St Dizier
Museum of Childhood, Bethnal Green (V and A)
Tibor Reich
Peter Richley
Sotheby's, Belgravia
Sotheby's, Chester
Tiatsa Toy Museum

We are grateful to White Mouse Editions Ltd for permission to reproduce figs in Appendix VI from pp 220–222 *The Art of the Tin Toy* by David Pressland, published by New Cavendish Books.

We have unfortunately been unable to trace the copyright holders of *Mechanical Tin Toys in Colour* by Arno Weltens (original Dutch title Mechanischblikken Speelgoed), published by Blandford Press, and would appreciate any information that would enable us to do so.

KEY TO SYMBOLS USED IN CAPTIONS

M   Mint. No damage. Factory fresh as made.

VP   Very fine. As above but exceptional.

S   Sunday. Complete and showing signs of only minimal use with adult supervision.

E   Enjoyed. Evidence of some wear, paint loss, minor accessories missing but acceptable to collector.

P   Playworn. Considerable evidence of use, dents and other damage, rusting, parts missing. Worth collecting only if scarce, cheap, and until a better example is found or missing parts turn up.

D   Distressed. As above, only worse.

I   Important.

R   Rare.

U   Unusual (rarely encountered or unusual to find a surviving example in this condition).

C   Commonplace (plenty of these to be found but still collectable).

CHAPTER ONE

EARLY TIN-PLATE TOYS TO 1914

EAGLE VERSUS EAGLE

It is, perhaps, no accident that the true birthplace of the modern toy industry was the ancient Bavarian city of Nuremberg. Its walls, turrets and gateways flanked by massive towers, narrow streets, and quaint gabled houses all date back centuries to when it was the gateway through which passed both the rich goods and the mysteries of the East, on their way to northern Germany.

In such an atmosphere, where the ideas and ideologies of East and West met and mingled, the arts and sciences both flourished. It was here that the artist Albrecht Dürer lived and worked; here that in 1649 Johannes Hautsch constructed a mechanical carriage propelled by men concealed within it (it was purchased by the Crown Prince of Sweden); and here that clockwork, the pocket watch, the thimble, the clarinet, the fire engine and the invalid carriage were all developed.

In fact, there would appear to be a direct connection between full-sized vehicles and toys in Nuremberg in the mid-1600s if we accept the likelihood that Gottfried Hautsch and his father were related to Johannes of the same name. Being blacksmiths in the city, they were responsible for the construction of over one hundred clockwork toy soldiers made for the Dauphin of France. Designed by a French architect, Sebastian de Vauban, they took four years to construct and could march and shoot their guns. Sadly they have not survived for posterity. By the time Gottfried died in 1703, he had become famous for the tin soldiers he made.

So, the connection with toymaking was already established, as were the skills of metal-working and the intricacies of clockwork, when, in 1815, the technique for pressing out shapes in sheet metal was discovered. Otto Senft tells us in his thesis *Die Metallspielwaren und der Spielwarenhandel von Nürnberg und Fürth* that the secrets of the process were passed by German labourers to Vienna in 1822, and were known and employed in Nuremberg only a few years later.

1

Certainly, in the 1826 catalogue of Johannes Karl Lenchs we find not only wooden, alabaster and pewter toys, but also some examples of tin plate, and it was in the same year that Mattheus Hess founded one of the oldest toy factories not only in Nuremberg but in Germany. His son Johann took over the running of the works in 1866 following the death of his father, and in later years the firm was to be prominent in the field of toy motor vehicles.

STARS AND STRIPES

It would be incorrect, however, to imagine that this early manufacturing activity was centred only on Nuremberg or, indeed, in Europe. The Americans were, if anything, quicker off the mark in the development of the tin toy than their European counterparts, if not first in the field.

By the 1830s, several toy factories were established in New England, and by 1838 Francis, Field and Francis had built a large factory in Philadelphia. From this period until virtually the end of the century the Americans were destined to dominate the market.

Their first clockwork toy appeared in 1856 – at least, it is the earliest documented example so far recorded – and was produced in Forestville by George W. Brown & Company. Brown had, appropriately (and with shades of Nuremberg), been apprenticed to a clockmaker, and the company included clocks among its products.

Locomotives, coaches and horse-trams accounted for most of the toy production, together with some paddle boats, but other household goods, including oil lamps, took precedence from 1862 onwards. In 1868 the company was taken over by Bristol Brass, but Brown obviously enjoyed making toys and, while retaining a shareholding in the latter company, started another toy factory – Stevens and Brown – in partnership with the brothers J. & B. Stevens.

Stevens and Brown were destined to produce not only tin-plate but also cast-iron toys (a medium favoured by many other American firms well into the twentieth century), some of which were mechanically propelled – an unusual combination. Although Brown died in 1889, the Stevens brothers carried on; we shall hear more of them in later chapters.

It would probably be true to say that, although the United States enjoyed a reasonably successful toy market until the outbreak of the Second World War, its influence greatly declined from about 1895 onwards, and was not destined to re-emerge until the late 1940s.

Why this should have been so is difficult to pinpoint, although the German industry was protected to a degree by government subsidies and cheaper transport and shipping costs, which made it difficult for other countries to compete. America's decline may mainly have been due, however, to a growing demand for more sophisticated toys, prompted by the German offerings.

During the 'Golden Age' of US tin-toy production – 1860–95 – the American toy was very much a reflection of the national temperament (as, indeed, was that from Germany). As such, it tended to be simpler in construction, less subtle in colouring, lighter and less ponderous than the serious German toys, and embodying a whimsicality which betrayed the closeness (which one would expect from so young a nation) of the indigenous folk-art.

Prominent during this burgeoning period were Althof, Bergmann & Co., founded in 1856 by the three Bergmann brothers, Edward Ives who powered his toys with clockwork supplied by the New Haven Clock Company, Merriam Manufacturing Company, Hull & Stafford, and James Fallows – but few of these exerted much influence after the turn of the century.

FRANCO-PRUSSIAN RIVALRY

It is significant, however, that by 1895 most of the German manufacturers who were destined to dominate the scene until the outbreak of the First World War had already established themselves, and with production greatly increased from the mid-1880s onwards they even eclipsed the more thrusting of the French firms. Of these, Fernand Martin's factory on the Boulevard Menilmontant employed, at times, over a hundred workers, and between 1878 and 1912 produced some 800,000 toys, many of which were sold by street pedlars and cheap stores (the Arts et Metiers Museum in Paris preserves a selection of these toys). The factory was eventually taken over by Bonnet et Cie. Radiquet (Radiquet et Massiot from 1889) was founded in 1872 and continued in production until 1905, and G. Dessin would appear (from surviving documentary evidence) to have exceeded the production of its German contemporaries, if only for a short period.

In conjunction with the greatly increased production of the German firms of the 1880s and 1890s came also a more universal adoption of the published manufacturer's catalogue as a means of promoting sales still further. In addition, such German wholesalers as Moses Kohnstam – an archetypal entrepreneur – inaugurated international toy fairs which gave further impetus to the expansion of the German industry.

The influence of the Kohnstam business, founded in the mid-1870s, and its successors, is found throughout all the periods covered by this book. Kohnstam also managed to straddle comfortably the contentious gulf between the tin-plate and die-cast toy producers and fanciers. Their Manchester Toy Week, forerunner of the Harrogate Toy Fair, extended their

3

sphere far beyond the environs of Fürth (their headquarters adjacent to Nuremberg) and consolidated the position of German manufacturers who had first exhibited in Britain in the Crystal Palace at the Great Exhibition of 1851.

THE NUREMBERG 'RING'

At that time, only two manufacturers of tin-plate toys were actually registered in Nuremberg, although there were probably several individuals carrying on business in a very small way. By 1861 the number had risen to an astounding 241 small factories, but as the total number of employees was only 360, it seems likely that many of them were merely working at home, assembling and hand-painting toys.

Whoever they were, we know little of them – in fact, very little information exists concerning even the more important German toymakers prior to 1890 – and their wares were probably distributed more or less locally to a largely indigenous market.

By 1900, however, Nuremberg was supporting some 1,120 people (half women) in the toy industry, and the number of firms had consolidated to a nevertheless creditable sixty-five. More significantly, this latter figure included such important names as Bing, Bub, Carette, Distler, Doll, Fleischmann, Günthermann, Hess, Mangold and Plank, all of whom were to be prominent in their individual portrayals of the motor vehicle, particularly during the next two or three decades.

MAKING THEIR MARK

The Trademarks Registration Act of 1875 in Great Britain, and similar legislation in other countries, was progressively reinforced, and produced a variety of effects not necessarily intended by its promoters. Its prime purpose was, of course, to prevent counterfeiting (and thus infringements of patents in some cases), cheap copies, and the misuse of trademarks, and in this it was partially successful. The benefits (from a collector's point of view) which also accrued, however, included the increasing incorporation of the trademark itself in the lithographic decoration of the toy, and a tendency towards greater individuality. These aspects are, of course, invaluable in the identification of toys and, since the trademarks altered from time to time, can also assist in dating.

Methods of production had become standardised very much earlier, however; and since they had changed little in the intervening years despite the introduction of more sophisticated machinery, it is perhaps worth examining in brief detail the principal stages involved in the manufacturing process. There were exceptions, of course, particularly after the canned food industry had established itself and provided a cheap source of tin plate to the semi-amateur home producer. In France and Germany (and presumably in America, too, where they 'eat all they can, and can all they can't') hundreds of part-timers collected tin scraps – particularly old food tins – and fashioned 'one-off' toys.

The ingenuity of the French when it comes to improvisation is second to none. Remember the incredibly detailed objects and toys fashioned from bone by French prisoners during the Napoleonic Wars? Prisoners in the Santé prison in France were later to echo this activity with toys made from tin scraps. But when the German makers adopted preprinted tin plate – c. 1890 – the day of the handmade toy was virtually at an end.

HANDWORK

Admittedly, certain processes were still carried out by hand – the transition of the original idea from sketch to final drawing and wooden prototype, of course, and the construction of master moulds, from that model, of every separate part of the toy. Thereafter, however, tinsmiths (using special presses) would press and cut the tin plate into the desired shapes and, where preprinting did not apply, female workers dipped the surfaces to be painted in tanks of lacquer.

Many of the early vehicles boasted separate drivers and passengers – sometimes constructed of tin plate, sometimes of plaster or composition material – and on these the facial detail was normally applied by hand. Similarly, the final assembly of the clockwork and the body of the toy was the province of a largely female workforce.

POWER SOURCES

Most manufacturers, particularly the German ones, favoured the 'slot and tab' assembly with which we are still familiar today, although the French tended to solder parts together. There were also differences in the methods of propulsion adopted. The heavy and bulky clockwork spring (which required space into which the spring could expand when wound down), inherited from the clockmaking industry, tended to be employed more frequently by the makers of toy locomotives, whereas makers of cars and trucks preferred the lighter (if less powerful) coil spring developed by Lehmann of Brandenberg and consisting of piano wire wound round a central cylinder with gearwheels, to take the drive, affixed at each end.

This difference was logical, since the toy locomotive usually ran on an endless track pulling carriages and trucks. It therefore needed a powerful spring, and one which would propel it for a reasonable distance. The toy car or truck, however, was invariably relegated to the floor, propelled only itself, and required only sufficient power to carry it in a straight line until its inevitable collision with the furniture.

Clockwork was, however, by no means universally incorporated in either toy locomotives or other vehicles – particularly those of the very small, cheap varieties – and the larger versions of these 'push-along' or 'pull-along' types are normally called 'carpet toys'.

As the full-sized motor vehicle became more sophisticated, however, and the arrangement of its mechanical parts standardised to a pattern originally laid down by Panhard – front-mounted engine beneath a bonnet, driving through a gear system to the rear wheels – its toy counterpart also became available in increasingly realistic form.

FOR SONS OF THE RICH

Perhaps no manufacturer captured the essence of the Edwardian motor car more completely than the Nuremberg-based firm of Georges Carette, while yet retaining the charm of the tin toy. Surviving examples are now so sought after by collectors that it is perhaps appropriate that we should discuss in some detail, and before the others, this great creative influence which so embodied and symbolised Nuremberg as the very crucible of what we now accept as 'the Art of the Tin Toy'.

Carette was French, as his name suggests; and although he married a German woman he always retained his French citizenship. He established himself in Nuremberg in 1886, relying initially on finance from the Hopf brewery family. Hopf had connections with Bing of Nuremberg who, commencing in 1863 as retailers, had been producing tin toys since 1879.

Initially, therefore, Georges Carette et Cie manufactured parts for Gebrüder Bing – mainly for the train sets for which Bing were already famous – but severed this connection in the early 1890s. Throughout the history of the toy manufacturers there are parallels to be drawn with their real-life contemporaries. Just as the Dodge Brothers commenced in business supplying Henry Ford, but eventually became his largest competitor, so too with Carette and Bing.

The shape of things to come was apparent when, in 1893, Carette showed an electric tram at the International Exhibition – the first toy manufacturer to do so – and probably the first significant vehicle to appear under Carette's own name. Wisely, however, he did not 'go it alone' totally at this stage.

His new partner, Paul Josephtal, also had connections, this time in England with Wenman Bassett-Lowke who, in 1899, formed Bassett-Lowke & Co. to manufacture model trains to the highest possible standards. From 1901 these were produced in conjunction with Carette and – coincidentally – Bing, who manufactured the more expensive models.

INTERNATIONAL CO-OPERATION

These activities are, however, beyond the scope of this book, but do show that Carette's early work was associated with those who, like himself, insisted on the highest degree of accuracy and quality. Anglo-German co-operation was, in fact, nothing new, since, despite the very considerable industrial resources existing in Germany, the Nuremberg toymakers (like the Americans) relied very largely upon South Wales for their supplies of tin plate.

Carette's range of cars covered the whole spectrum from a small two-seater (with driver in painted tin-plate or 'dressed' in fabric) up to a four-seater tonneau, landaulette and enclosed limousine, and even in this ulti-mate form was offered in a bewildering selection of wheelbases and detail finishes.

The three basic wheelbase sizes offered in 1911 were 22 cm, 32 cm and 40 cm, but even the smallest of these was available *to wholesalers* in four quality variations with (in Britain) a lower and upper price limit of 1s. 9d. and 7s. 4d. respectively (pre-decimal currency). Of these, the three cheapest boasted lithographic detail, while the 7s. 4d. model was hand enamelled.

Retailers' prices would, of course, have been considerably higher than those quoted – say, a 50 per cent mark up or more – but even so they are mouth-watering when compared with the thousands of pounds which a good, original, boxed Carette can command today.

Five distinct options were offered on the 32 cm wheelbase, however, all of which were improvements on the basic metal-wheeled lithographed type with straightforward clockwork mechanism and plain sidelamps at 5s. (25p). For an extra pre-decimal 8d. the wholesaler could obtain reverse gear, and 2s. (10p) above the basic would provide the luxury of glass windows for the enclosed limousine compartment, and more detailed sidelamps. Nine shill-ings (45p) purchased rubber tyres and a nickelled radiator shell, and the most expensive model in this middle range boasted hand-enamelling, four nickel-plated lamps, rubber tyres and detail moulded front seats, a compo-sition (not tin-plate) driver and a roof held in position by studs and nuts rather than tabs and slots. For these additional refinements the total whole-sale price was just £1!

The long wheelbase version could also be obtained with similar options, but with the most expensive type available with footman, extra fold-down or 'jump' seats in the rear compartment, a wire rack on the roof to accom-modate hat boxes and luggage, and additional running-board supports.

Strangely, Carette eschewed trademarks on all but the hand-enamelled versions on all three wheelbases, honouring the shortest (22 cm) of these with the largest and most prominent logo. Possibly this was the most popular of all the models, appealing to the *nouveau riche* and merchant classes, while the most expensive (40 cm) model would have been the preserve of royalty and the nobility, to whom a prominent trademark would have given offence.

Certainly, it is by these various limousine models that Carette is best known and remembered, and it is examples of these which, of all Carette's vehicles, have survived in the greatest numbers. It is scarcely surprising that this should be so, since the Carette was truly the 'Rolls-Royce' of toys. Experience has shown that, generally speaking, the odds against a real motor car surviving, in good condition, into preservation are directly related to the amount invested in it in the first place. And so it is with toys. Quite apart from anything else, we do know that many Carette cars were purchased for adults – usually coinciding with the purchase of a full-size limousine – and were therefore spared the vicissitudes of the nursery. The homes of the rich tended, also, to be better ordered than those of the poor, with a Nanny to supervise the nursery, and this improved the survival rate. In large houses, discarded objects tend to be relegated to attics and cellars, stables and outbuildings, rather than be thrown away; whereas the pressure on space in smaller establishments leaves less room for hoarding.

All these things have contributed to the rich legacy of Carette toys which have been (and are still being) discovered. But might we not attribute their longevity to the simple pride of possession felt by even the most boisterous Edwardian youngster upon unwrapping, with trembling fingers, that Christmas so long ago, the jewel for the purchase of which even father's motives were suspect?

PENNY FOR 'EM . . .

Having examined the zenith, as it were, let us then briefly take a look at the other end of the scale, to those ephemeral and for the most part short-lived trifles which gladdened, for just a few brief hours, the hearts of poorer children. I refer to the 'penny' toys (1d.) which once could be found on every pedlar's tray and in every cheap bazaar.

If Carette was the 'Rolls-Royce' of toys, then the 'penny' toy was, I suppose, the 'Model "T" Ford' or the 'Bullnose Morris', made in enormous numbers at very low cost. Generally speaking, however, motor cars are more durable than toys, and children more demanding than the most careless driver. In addition, motor cars have a utility value which extends their lives beyond their makers' original intentions, and toys do not.

While, therefore, the numbers in which they were produced should have ensured, like the Model 'T' Ford, a healthy survival rate, the 'penny' toy is now far more rarely encountered in good condition than its expensive counterpart, and a pristine example commands a price totally out of proportion to its initial cost.

On the credit side, they are smaller, more easily stored and concealed (and thus still being discovered), but one cannot escape the fact that the vast majority were trodden underfoot, left in the gutter or garden to rust away or, having lost a wheel, burned with Christmas wrappings – just one small part of the inevitable debris of the festivities.

And yet, the 'penny' toy has a charm all its own. The very flimsiness and crudity of its construction, and the budget to which it was produced, dictated a degree of clever interpretation combined with an economy of detail which in cases bordered on genius. At least, they were colourful, naïve and cheerful; at most, true art.

Although examples can be found from later periods, the true 'penny' toy – costing one penny – enjoyed a heyday of just about twenty years until the outbreak of the First World War in 1914. In most cases, these toys came, like their larger cousins, from in and around Nuremberg, and they were exported in large numbers all over the world.

Specific designs were often sold to specific markets (a practice of some of the manufacturers of the larger toys – Lehmann in particular), and so one finds a 'General' double decker bus for the London market, a Postes et Telegraphes van for Paris, or a London taxi complete with 'For Hire' sign among those of more international appeal.

Penny toys were made by Kellermann, Distler, Einfalt, Fischer, Essdee and G.L.B. (Italy) among others, but by far the most prolific manufacturer from the pre-First World War period was J. Ph. Meier. Johann Phillip Meier founded his company as early as 1879 in Nuremberg, and in 1894 registered his trademark of a dog pulling a small cart. Despite the modest nature of his products, Meier's output was such that during the Edwardian period his company became one of the leading Nuremberg firms, with a worldwide export trade largely controlled by such wholesalers as Moses Kohnstam. Meier's toys can be identified by either a crude rendering of the 'dogcart' logo lithographed or embossed on the metal, or by the monogram 'J.Ph.M.', 'JPM', 'JM', or simply 'M'.

Apart from Marks Penny Bazaar (now Marks & Spencer) and similar emporiums, penny toys were widely sold by street vendors, given away by rag-and-bone merchants in exchange for rags or scrap metal, and sold in sites favoured by market traders. In London Lowther Arcade in the Strand and Ludgate Hill were both popular. Wholesalers were able to conduct brisk business selling toys by the gross (144) for 8s. (40p.)! At a derisory penny each, penny toys provided enterprising street traders with a useful 50 per cent profit and no shortage of customers.

Today, representative collections of penny toys are maintained by David Pressland and Patrick Rylands (the former now being associated with Allen Levy of the London Toy Museum, which is well worth a visit), and the Victoria and Albert Museum preserves the Ernst King collection at Bethnal Green.

9

Having dealt with the sublime and the 'gor'blimey', what of that broad band of 'middle of the road' toymakers for Mr Everyman's child? Well, we commenced with Nuremberg and, since that city exerted the greatest influence on toy vehicle manufacturers at least until 1914, it would perhaps be instructive to look at some of the other companies that once flourished there.

NOT ALWAYS CLOCKWORK

As we have seen, Hess were in the vanguard of the very earliest makers and are notable for both the high quality of their lithography (a quality which they shared with Carette) and the very individual method of propulsion to which they largely adhered right into the 1920s.

This consisted of a heavy lead flywheel usually concealed (in the case of cars) beneath the bonnet and mounted on a spindle, the end of which projected through a hole in the side and revolved in contact with the upper surface of the circumference of the wheel. The flywheel was actuated, appropriately, by a prominent 'starting handle' projecting forward at the front – just where you would expect to find such a device on a real motor car – and although conventional clockwork appeared on a few models, it is with these flywheel-propelled types that Hess established their reputation. The cars often carried the legend 'Hessmobil' in addition to the 'H' or 'JLH' (adopted after Johann took over from his father in 1866), and the family remained in control of the company until Johann died in 1934.

STEAM TOO

Peter Doll, although a tinsmith, was primarily a producer of steam engines and accessories, and when in 1898 he formed Doll et Cie with J. Sondheim, it was in that field that the company concentrated. Another partner, Max Bein, joined the company in the period shortly before the First World War, resulting in a line of clockwork novelty toys which was continued, together with complete steam vehicles, following the armistice.

MASS PRODUCTION

We have already touched on the activities of Gebrüder Bing (or Nürnberger Metall- und Lackierwaarenfabrik Gebrüder Bing, to give them their full title) in connection with Carette, but the company actually commenced business in 1863 as a wholesaler of household goods and toys, and did not actually manufacture on its own account until 1879.

The company was at that time under the control of Ignaz and Adolph Bing, and expanded rapidly. In many ways, Bing were similar to Märklin – established a hundred miles from Nuremberg at Göppingen – and both companies concentrated at first on toy trains. It was not long, however, before Bing moved into cars, ships, steam engines, hot-air motors, magic lanterns and optical and electrical items, and it was this over-diversification which probably brought about their eventual downfall.

During the period covered in this chapter, however, Bing flourished, even at one stage introducing a limousine calculated to compete with Carette's masterpiece. Hans Eberl, one of the lesser known Nuremberg manufacturers, also produced a limousine, as did Märklin, although both of these are extremely rare. Examples of Bing's attempt to beat Carette at their own game are also rarely encountered, and somehow they lack that combination of reality and fantasy which made the Carette so successful.

Bing's greatest success was in the cheaper toys, which included an enormous variety of vehicles. A passable representation of a coal scuttle-bonneted De Dion Bouton two-seater endured from about 1910 until well into the late 1920s, and illustrates a facet of toy collecting which can be misleading. Children are, by nature, conservative. They love repetition, never tire of the same favourite stories, and will remain faithful as a group to a popular toy. As a result, many of Bing's toys (and those of other manufacturers) remained in production for long periods with only detail changes in design or construction. Frequently, therefore, a toy vehicle may appear to be of earlier date than is, in fact, the case, and it is only by close scrutiny and comparison with catalogues that accurate dating can be approached, if not achieved. Obviously, every manufacturer hopes for a 'long run', since it is on the strength of these hardy perennials that a company can afford to diversify into new designs.

ALTER EGO

Bing's open four-seater tourer was very popular, and also poses something of a mystery since it appeared in England during the same period wearing the trademark of Brimtoy. Founded just before the First World War, Brimtoy did not long enjoy an independent existence, amalgamating with Wells (of whom we shall say more later) in the 1930s. It seems likely, however, that despite the legend 'Brimtoy Brand. British Make' which their toys bore, they were in fact made by Bing.

Obviously the First World War put a stop to such co-operation, but such cross-pollination of ideas, designs and makes was fairly common and, indeed, still is, and we encounter it again in the case of some die-cast vehicles in the appropriate chapter. It is also obvious when comparing

11

surviving examples of vehicles from rival manufacturers that a degree of copying and plagiarism was not unknown.

Although they appealed to the lower priced market, however, Bing and Märklin's products were always of the highest quality, and of the two, Bing appear to have made many more road vehicles, and thus to be better represented among the survivors.

LEHMANN AND GÜNTHERMANN

Two other manufacturers who tend to be considered together by collectors are Lehmann and Günthermann, and although it was not until 1951 that Lehmann eventually moved to Nuremberg, their products, like those of Günthermann, were so representative of the quality associated with that city that we will look at both makes side by side.

Of the two, Lehmann were the older company, commencing business under the aegis of Ernst Paul Lehmann of Brandenberg in 1881. Initially, flywheel mechanisms, similar to those employed by Hess, powered their toys, but the coil spring was later developed and perfected.

Lehmann's cousin, Johann Richter, joined the company in 1911, in which year the trademark was altered to combine Ernst Paul's initials into a single monogram within the distinctive border of a bookbinder's press. When Lehmann died in 1934, Richter took over and, because of material shortages in those depression-ridden days, a cheaper range of small toys under the series name of 'Gnome' was introduced.

Like Günthermann, Lehmann produced many novelty toys in the period up to 1914, and of these several were vehicles. Worth mentioning, and a prize for any collector, is Lehmann's *Li-La*, or *The Auto Sisters*, a motorised hansom cab wherein sit the two sisters. On a platform in front sits a dog, while aloft at the rear sits the red-coated and top-hatted cabby. As the cab moves forward, the dog turns its head from side to side, while the two sisters attempt to dislodge it by beating it with their umbrellas. To complete the little charade, the cabby, smilingly unaware of this drama, steers the equipage on a drunken course.

Naughty Boy and Uncle consists of an early representation of a *vis-à-vis* car in which uncle and nephew face one another. The boy is endeavouring to steer the car, and receives intermittent slaps from uncle for his presumption. Yet another, three-wheeled car transports uncle on a world tour while he raises and lowers his hat. Behind him, a Blackamoor twirls a parasol aloft.

It will be seen, therefore, that in depicting not only the fledgling motor vehicles of the early Edwardian period, but also the humorous (and sometimes absurd) elements of human nature, the toys were not only marginally educational, but also highly ingenious.

Not all Lehmann's toys were of a novelty nature, however, and as the motor car itself gained acceptance, so increasingly did the toys adopt a 'straight' role, and the humour (if any) was relegated to the driver and occupants rather than to the vehicle itself.

THE COPIERS

Imitation is the sincerest form of flattery, and Walter Stock's company founded in 1905 became well known for its Lehmann copies. Stock & Co. were based not in Nuremberg but in Solingen, and the quality of their finish and lithography was never up to Lehmann standards. Lehmann also enjoyed the doubtful privilege of having their trademark plagiarised by H. Yamada of Japan; doubtful because the open touring car which it graced was pretty well a carbon copy of Günthermann's tourer of 1912!

The quality of construction, printing and colour finish of the Japanese offering, however, was such that it is difficult to understand why the reputation of the Japanese was not established much earlier. In fact, for many years the Japanese were known only for producing cheap, inferior copies of European toys.

S. Günthermann commenced tin-plate toy manufacture in Nuremberg in 1877, and died in 1890. He left two sons, Christian and Leonard, and a widow who very shortly remarried. Her new partner, Arnold Weigel, continued and expanded the business, concentrating particularly upon exports to the USA, and as early as 1914 no less than 65 per cent of the company's output was sold there.

After 1900 Günthermann's range was heavily oriented towards road vehicles, and these often compared favourably in quality with those of Lehmann. Frequently they pursued the same theme too, and there is, for example, little to choose between the horseless carriages offered by both firms in 1906.

CATALOGUES

A full range of passenger cars (and even double-decker buses) was offered, many of them marketed in England by Benetfinks of Cheapside and Gamages of Holborn, Harrods and Gamleys. In addition to the manufacturers' catalogues, we can also rely upon the catalogues produced by these retailers for the identification and dating of models, although, of course, manufacturers' names were rarely quoted.

These early toys were, almost without exception, simple representations of motor vehicles rather than scaled-down copies of any particular make, and while it is possible to liken Carette's limousines to a Brasier or large

Talbot, and Lehmann's hansom does bear some relation to a freak motor-ised hansom made by Vauxhall, it was not until after the First World War that individual marques could be identified.

We have already commented on the decline in the influence of the American toymakers after 1900, and the fact that so much of Günthermann's production found its way to America speaks for itself. It would be quite wrong, however, to dismiss the Americans out of hand. During the period under review, the Ferdinand Strauss Corporation of New York were famed for their Strauss Mechanical Toys, and included in their range of vehicles examples which were every bit the equal of their European competitors. Their Interstate Bus, which dates from *c.* 1912/14, is typical, but is nowadays a rarity even in its native America. The company later became Strauss, Man & Co., and after 1920 was taken over by Louis Marx, who was to prove a dominant force for three decades.

PERFIDE ALBION

As a glance at contemporary British catalogues will show, the contribution made by English firms during this period was small as far as road vehicles were concerned, although firms like Hornby and Bassett-Lowke set new standards in the model train world. Brimtoy have already been mentioned, but one Birmingham maker, who later moved to London, is especially worthy of mention.

Burnett Ltd, with their trademark of St George and the Dragon, were responsible for some of the very best British toys made up to 1914, and again in the 1920s, and their *c.* 1910 open-drive landaulette taxi, complete with chauffeur (registered BL 912), is comparable with (or arguably better than) anything made by Carette.

Bearing in mind, however, the indigenous pool of skilled metal workers in the British industrial Midlands and the availability of tin plate from South Wales, it is something of a mystery that the British toy did not flourish alongside the burgeoning Midlands car and motorcycle industries, but such is the case.

Whiteley Tansley & Co. of Liverpool made toys under the Whitanco trademark incorporating a motor wheel, and confined their small output almost exclusively to road vehicles. They started late, however, not regis-tering their trademark until 1916, and little was heard of them after the war, although the quality was good and the vehicles attractive in appearance.

The boom in France at the end of the nineteenth century proved to be short-lived, and many of the early firms like Radiquet did not survive the world trade slump of 1907. Charles Roitel's firm, founded in 1880, was, however, active until about 1920 and made some cars, but the use of the founder's initials 'C.R.' as a trademark leads to confusion with the older (and subsequently longer lived) Paris company of Charles Rossignol.

TAXI DE LA MARNE

Rossignol's approach to tin-plate toy manufacture was highly individual, and in some cases paradoxical. While on the one hand much of their lithography verged on caricature and was more concerned with overall creative effect rather than with any resemblance to the real-life object portrayed, their Renault taxi was recognisable as such. Not only this, but it was readily identifiable with the 'Taxi de la Marne', the famous vehicle that was used during the Battle of the Marne and probably turned the tide of the First World War. Incidentally, some sources quote Rossignol's full name as Roitel-Rossignol, so there may be a connection between the two firms.

A NOTABLE CASUALTY OF THE WAR

Important though these French, British and American makers were, the fact remains that it was Germany who really called the tune throughout the first two decades of the twentieth century. By the outbreak of war in 1914, the original ten manufacturers listed earlier in this chapter (see page 4) as being established in Nuremberg had added to their ranks Eberl (1902), Ettinger (1907), G. Fischer (1903), H. Fischer (1908), Kellermann (1910), Kienberger/Huki/Kico (1910), Müller & Kadeder (1900), Schuco/Schreyer (1912), Rissmann (1912), Tipp (1912) and a host of other lesser known names.

Virtually all of these were destined to expand and survive the war. The only significant casualty among the German toy firms (in Nuremberg and elsewhere) was Georges Carette. As we have seen, Carette chose to retain his French citizenship, although he lived in Germany, and for this reason was forced to flee when war was declared. Paul Josephtal endeavoured to keep the company going, but inevitably the factory eventually closed – in 1917 – never to reopen. Carette unfortunately died in France during the 1920s, so there was no possibility of a resumption of production, but another Nuremberg factory, that of Karl Bub, did perpetuate some Carette items. The two companies had worked closely, producing some toys in common, and Bub continued to list some of these well after 1917.

The holocaust which followed the events at Sarajevo, when the heir to the throne of Austro-Hungary was assassinated by a Serbian fanatic, devastated France and Belgium and altered the map of Europe. Kingdoms fell, democracies and dictatorships arose, new frontiers appeared. The old order was destroyed.

This rather playworn three-quarter landaulette taxi was made by the Nuremberg company of H. Fischer, and bears their 'fish' trademark. It is unusual in that the folding hood is of real leather. Although showing its age, and missing both sidelamps and other small accessories, it retains its taximeter (to the driver's left) and the magenta/yellow paintwork with its black lining and royal blue running boards is still bright and colourful. P, R.

Fischer's answer to Georges Carette was this handsome open-drive limousine offered in various liveries, including cream with blue lining and roof, and gold surrounds to doors and roof rack (as with this example). As can be seen, the wheels are adjustable for steering, the vehicle is powered by clockwork and the two carriage lamps between the driver's and passengers' compartments are missing. E, R.

Both Lehmann and Günthermann offered variations on the 'Horseless Carriage' theme shortly after the turn of the century. These examples are from Günthermann, the open car of the *vis-à-vis* type with a small girl in the passenger seat and father's hand on the steering wheel, while the brougham lithographed in chocolate and yellow carries its driver precariously on a box at the front in the manner of contemporary electric vehicles. In each case the tyres are of rubber, E, R.

This charming and simple German truck, together with its load of potatoes and uniformed driver, was made *c.* 1910 by Gebrüder Bing of Nuremberg, and is typical of the high quality of German toys during the Edwardian period. Powered by clockwork it has rubber tyres and a working handbrake. S, R. (Museum of Childhood)

17

American toys of the nineteenth century were often delicate and attractive, if naïve, which is more than can be said for this friction-driven rear-entrance tonneau of about 1905. Made in heavy gauge metal, it probably emanates from the Clark factory who (like many other US manufacturers) adopted friction drive as being both cheap and robust. Dayton were another prominent American espouser of friction drive. E, R. (Museum of Childhood)

Brimtoy registered their 'Nelson's Column' trademark in 1914, just before the First World War, and these two carpet toys (pull-along rather than clockwork) are typical of their pre-war range. The open tourer is virtually identical to a similar car made by Bing, however, and there is some speculation as to whether Brimtoy were the manufacturers. Brimtoy amalgamated with Wells in 1932. S, R.

A variation on the open-drive limousine theme, this example is unmarked and of cheap construction, but is believed to be German in origin. Rear windows are lithographed on the tin, and there is no windscreen, but lining and bonnet detail are attractive. It probably dates from about 1911, and could be based on either a Charron or Renault taxi. E, R.

A handsome Lehmann 'Baldur' taxi in yellow and black but lacking its flag and taximeter. Lehmann tended to give their toys individual names, and this one dates from about 1914 or possibly later. The pretty little rear entrance tonneau on the right is certainly German, but carries no maker's identity – a situation often encountered even with the larger manufacturers. It dates from about 1910 but depicts a vehicle current in 1904/5. E, R.

Smoker's companion sets in the form of vehicles have for many years been popular. This beautiful little model of a steam Merryweather fire engine was designed to hold cigarettes and matches, and is a very early example. It is a presentation piece and its inscription 'Presented to Major Joicey, Xmas 1891' gives us the date. M, I.

When Georges Carette ceased production in 1917, some of his designs were taken over by Karl Bub of Nuremberg. The two firms had always worked closely together, and it is sometimes difficult to differentiate between examples (unmarked) from the two factories. This clockwork open-drive limousine was offered by both firms, but this example is attributed to Bub since it was found with its original box; *c.* 1910. M, I.

This delicate little filigree car is made entirely from silver wire and dates from about 1903. A gem like this would be a real 'find', but is unlikely to turn up outside a jeweller's shop. A mere 4 in. (10.2 cm) in length it was probably made by a jeweller as a present to the owner of a similar full-sized rear entrance tonneau. M, R.

The idea of decorated tins and containers is not new, and this car-shaped biscuit tin from Huntley & Palmer dates from just after the turn of the century. Many tins like this are still in use, particularly in the homes of the elderly, and can also be obtained cheaply at jumble sales. Most of the detail on this tin is lithographed, but there is some embossing, and the wheels turn separately. P, R. (Peter Richley Collection)

The 'Rolls-Royce' of Edwardian toys was undoubtedly the Nuremberg-built Georges Carette, in whatever form it appeared. The limousine illustrated here came in a large variety of liveries and degrees of luxury on three separate wheelbases, but even in its most spartan form was still magnificent. Loosely based on the Brasier of the period (c. 1910), this model has bevelled glass windows, opening rear doors, roof rack, forward and reverse gears and adjustable steering. S, I.

Another contrast in tin plate. The early lorry by Johann Distler is German and dates from around 1914, while the Ford Model 'Y' is one of the Tri-ang Minic range, made in Britain, and produced in the 1930s. Distler were one of the main producers of 'penny' toys in Germany both before and after the First World War. Both examples can be seen in the Tiatsa Toy Museum in Stratford. S, R (lorry); S, U (car).

Another novelty toy from Lehmann. Called by its makers 'Tut Tut' (Toot Toot), it featured a lithographed car with hand-painted driver. This generously proportioned gentleman blew his horn while the car steered an erratic course. The steering mechanism was ingeniously linked under the car to a small bellows to produce the overall effect; c.1910. M, R.

One of the most popular of the Edwardian Bing toys was this two-seater runabout based loosely on the contemporary Mercedes. It was also offered as a more luxurious four-seater side-entrance tonneau, but in the cheaper two-seater range also appeared in De Dion guise. This latter type was made from about 1910 until the late 1920s, which makes exact dating difficult. S, R.

Lehmann also fielded an open tourer in the period immediately before the First World War, and this 'Panne' version is a cheap clockwork toy without either wings, running board or lamps (see illustration on original box lid). Günthermann's version (with wings and lamps) was plagiarised by the Japanese firm H. Yamada, but it was Lehmann's trademark which the Japanese placed on the bonnet! M, R.

Typical of the novelty toys produced by Lehmann of Brandenberg during the Edwardian period is this 'Naughty Boy and Uncle'. Featuring an early *vis-à-vis* veteran car with tiller steering, it is clearly marked with the Lehmann name, and patents are also prominently listed. The boy attempts to steer the car and receives an occasional slap from uncle for his pains; *c.*1910. M, R.

This four-seater side-entrance tonneau is in remarkably good condition for its age (about 1908) and is complete with both chauffeur and rear seat passengers. Driven by clockwork it is as yet unidentified, although the rear passenger door carries a distinctive 'Y' or 'J' logo. Finished in cream and lined in red and gold, it is most attractive, and has a lever at the front for adjusting the steering. S, R.

One of the earliest of Günthermann's automobile toys, and issued in competition with Bing's 'Spyder', this delicate little *vis à vis* dates from about 1900 and is 25 cm in length. In many ways it is more a model than a toy, and displays none of the exuberance of the novelty toys which were to become so popular in the next decade. S, I.

Two periods are represented by these two tin-plate toys. The Lehmann delivery van, complete with working roller blind, is pre-First World War (probably about 1910) while the large six-cylinder saloon dates from the mid-1920s. It was offered under the Moko label (i.e. Moses Kohnstam), but Moko were a sales organisation only. The mechanism is interesting in that all six pistons undulate in turn, ringing the small bells. Probably by Mangold. S, R.

Günthermann of Nuremberg also produced novelty toys during the period up to 1914, and this stylised clown car is typical. Some 15.8 cm long, it incorporates a clown driver who, geared to the mechanism, jumps up and down alternately losing and regaining his 'wig'; c. 1907. S, R.

CHAPTER TWO

TIN PLATE IN THE TWENTIES AND THIRTIES

Because collectors of tin-plate toys and those interested in die casts and other types tend to divide into two camps, the chapters in this book have been designed to separate the development stories of both. In order to gain a proper perspective, therefore, this chapter and that dealing with post-war tin-plate developments should be read in conjunction with the final chapter, which covers the die-cast scene.

BETWEEN THE WARS

The long summer of the Edwardian era was over, and the armistice of 1918 ushered in a new and scarcely elegant age. But for all the ferocity of the conflict and the millions of lives lost, the fact remains that three of the principal protagonists – Germany, Britain and America – emerged with their territory and their factories physically unscathed.

The war had, indeed, increased the industrial capacity of all involved nations and had speeded up the adoption of mass-production techniques and the employment of cheap female labour. With the cancellation of war contracts, there followed an urgent need to fill the empty factories with work and, as a result, many new manufacturing activities were embarked upon.

GERMANY OVERCOMES HER PROBLEMS

In the atmosphere of optimism which prevailed in the heady days of 1919/20, toys were perhaps a natural antidote to the memory of the horrors of war, and new toy firms proliferated both in France and Germany, and to a lesser extent in Britain and America. Admittedly, Germany had to cope with galloping inflation, resulting in the collapse of the Mark in 1922, and, perhaps more importantly, with anti-German feeling among those countries which had been its best pre-war customers.

It appears to have coped admirably with both. Despite the fact that most German toy factories had been turned over to munitions work, they were quickly reconverted and the effervescent Messrs Kohnstam rapidly re-established themselves as wholesalers to the world. Prior to 1914 they had operated from Milan, Brussels and London, as well as from Germany, but all this had been swept away by the tide of war, and the London business had been expropriated under the Trading with the Enemy Acts. J. Kohnstam Ltd was, however, reconstituted and was soon once again importing Meier's penny toys into London.

The effects of mass production were not immediately felt, however, and echoing their full-size contemporaries in the motor car industry, many toy vehicles produced up to 1920 were hastily reissued pre-1915 designs. After 1920, however, the true post-war toys emerged.

JUST LIKE DADDY'S

They were less complex, perhaps, than their forebears, and more lightly (and therefore cheaply) constructed. In the case of toy vehicles, there was also a growing realisation among manufacturers that children, like their parents, were not oblivious to marque loyalty. The child, therefore, whose father was fortunate enough to own a Delaunay-Belleville, was likely to covet the toy version of one of these, and the Parisian firm of JEP (*Jouets de Paris*) provided one. They also made a superb Rolls-Royce dual cowl phaeton, a closed and open Renault, and a Panhard et Levassor.

It is perhaps misleading to quote these examples, however, since JEP's superbly engineered toys were neither light nor cheap, and were such good replicas that they were really more models than toys. They also did not become available until later in the decade. Certainly they lacked the naïve charm of the German products of which Bing's Model 'T' Ford was typical.

Bing, like Henry Ford, had the right idea. They reasoned – probably quite correctly – that if fifteen million adults were purchasing Model 'T' Fords, then the offspring of those fifteen million would also probably want their own version. They made no less than five differently bodied 'T' Ford types – a *charabanc*, a truck, a two-seater, a four-seater tourer and a Tudor coupé. Distler also jumped on the bandwagon with a one-ton van version which could be ordered from the factory with lithographed adverts on the sides to suit the purchaser!

HITLER AND THE JEWS

Although the 1920s were good years for Distler, 1923 brought the death of the founder, Johann, and the firm continued under the direction of Messrs Braun and Meyer. Braun and Meyer were both Jews and with the rise of National Socialism in Germany during the early 1930s and the accession of Hitler to the Chancellorship in 1933, they found it impossible to continue operations, and fled to England. The company continued, however, under the control of Ernst Volk, who later took over Trix.

This is perhaps a convenient point at which to examine the effect of Hitler's racial policies on the German toy industry. In both Britain and Germany the toy industry had, and has, a strong Jewish involvement. In Britain, of course, this has continued uninterrupted but in Germany it was brutally broken. The 'Aryan' replacements for the Jewish owners, managers and salesmen were rarely as competent as those they supplanted and, like much other cultural and industrial endeavour in Germany at the time, the industry declined.

The firm of Georg Levy is a typical example. Until 1916 (some sources quote 1910), Levy was a partner with Hubert Kienberger in the business carried on under the latter name, and started his own firm in 1920. A number of attractive, if rather crude, tin-plate vehicles were offered during the 1920s and early 1930s, but in 1934 political pressure forced his retirement and he settled in England. The company continued with the title of the Nürnberger Blechspielwarenfabrikation (Nuremberg Tin Toys Factory) under the management of Karl Ochs, but closed down in 1971.

A former employee of Carette, Joseph Falk, set up his business in 1897 and expanded his range by taking over some of the lines previously made by Schönner (the only notable Nuremberg bankruptcy of the period, in 1906). In 1935 he was forced to sell out to Ernst Plank, also of Nuremberg, or face forfeiture of his assets. Plank themselves lasted little longer before, in financial difficulty, they were absorbed by Schaller Brothers, who specialised in home-movie equipment.

The factories of Josef Kraus (Fandor toys) and Wilhelm Kraus (the two are often confused) were also the target for Nazi oppression. Josef (his toys took their name from the first three letters of the names of his mother and aunt, Fanny and Dora!) emigrated to the United States in 1933, and both factories were taken over by another Nuremberg firm, Keim & Co., well known for simple clockwork trains until 1960. However, both Kraus and Krauss factories closed for good in 1938.

A relative latecomer, Adolf Schuhmann, established his company in 1925 and suffered the same fate during the late 1930s, having held on longer than most; but most significant, in more ways than one, was the case of Tipp & Co.

PHOENIX FROM THE ASHES

Tipp were founded in 1912 in Nuremberg, the firm's name deriving from a Miss Tipp, one of the original directors. In 1919, control passed to the Jewish Ullmann family, with Philipp Ullmann at the helm, and they were forced to leave the country in 1933. The company was taken over and managed by Ernst Horn (a former director of Bing) and became famous for military toys and a toy version of Hitler's Grosser Mercedes (a situation unlikely to have arisen had the Ullmann family remained!). The Ullmanns came to England, however, and founded Mettoy. This company commenced production of tin-plate toys, and was successful, flourishing in the remaining years of the 1930s in its adopted home.

The militaristic influence of the Hitler regime had a profound effect even at nursery level in Germany, and with the ideas of National Socialism being instilled into youngsters through the medium of the Hitler Youth, it is hardly surprising that certain firms like Tipp (following expropriation), Lineol and Hausser should have concentrated on a military theme with their toys.

It is perhaps only natural that while such toys should find favour within Germany, their reception in other countries where Nazism was seen to be abhorrent was less enthusiastic. Towards the end of the 1930s, therefore, Germany's international influence declined, and the world export markets began to be invaded by American firms like Kingsbury (famous for their patent sealed-unit clockwork motor) and Louis Marx, although the latter company's British subsidiary in Dudley took care of most of the British market.

RISING SUN

Japan too, having managed to keep its war plans very much under wraps – unlike Germany's growing belligerence – attracted no similar adverse criticism of its internal politics and increased its share of the world tin-plate market, albeit at the cheap end of the trade.

BUYING AND SELLING IN BULK

One aspect of the 1920s and 1930s which deserves mention, however, was the influence on the manufacturers by the larger jobbing firms, retail chains, larger single shops (we have already mentioned Gamages and Harrods), and, particularly in America, the mail-order catalogue companies. The combined purchasing power of these bodies and the bulk orders that they were able to place enabled the toy firms to plan their production runs and budget their finances well in advance, and the timing of the appearance of the respective catalogues (very much like the timing of the annual Motor Shows for real motor vehicles) dictated the schedule leading up to the announcement of new models for the coming season.

Prominent among those who placed bulk orders in the United States were Wannamaker's, G. Sommers & Co. of St Paul, Minnesota, Baltimore Bargain House, Montgomery Ward, Sears Roebuck, Edward K. Tryon & Co. of Philadelphia, N. Shure & Co., and Charles William Stores.

Additionally, however, these outlets could also stipulate the kind of toys they wished the manufacturers to make, and frequently controlled the trade names under which the toys were sold. Thus, Butler Brothers of New York controlled 'Sampson' steel trucks; George Borgfeldt & Co. similarly guided 'Oh! Boy' toy vehicles, and Rieman Seabrey & Co. offered another similarly controlled steel truck line. All rather like the supermarkets today with their 'own brand' goods.

NOT ALWAYS WHAT THEY SEEM

This rather confusing situation – in which one manufacturer made toys under more than one brand name, or another so-called manufacturer was but a thinly disguised selling organisation – was, of course, of no interest to toy buyers at the time. It is only with the growth of interest in toy and model collecting that such niceties engage the attention of purchasers.

The trend which started with the Nuremberg companies before the First World War, whereby seemingly unconnected companies had marketing agreements either to make under licence or to sell ready-made certain of each other's toy lines, gained momentum in the 1930s and was destined to reach its peak after the Second World War.

D I Y

One particularly successful development from the tin-plate toy industry was the construction kit. One of the earliest makers of these was Structo Manufacturing Co. of Freeport, Illinois, whose excellent heavy steel 'Auto-builder' outfit included clockwork motors and working transmissions as early as 1917. Their slogan was 'Structo Toys make Men of Boys'! But unfortunately the company had reverted to steel carpet toys only by the early 1930s, by which time W. Butcher & Sons of London were offering their Primus Engineering Motor Chassis Outfit.

Stephan Bing, Oppenheimer and Erlanger, having taken over Förtner and Haffner in 1927, formed Trix, and although tin-plate toys were made initially, they introduced a metal construction kit of the same name in 1935. Bing also opened a British Trix subsidiary at the same time.

The British firm of Chad Valley, although founded in 1897 by Joseph Johnson of Harborne (near which flows the River Chad), did not produce tin-plate toys until the 1930s, and in 1936 achieved great success with their Ubilda car construction kit. Made from an aluminium alloy, the kit was continued until the war, and then reintroduced in an enlarged range in 1948.

Hornby of Liverpool had, of course, also offered a construction toy (initially called Mechanics Made Easy) from 1901 and renamed Meccano in 1907. Although it was possible to construct a motor car from the components in the kit, it was not until 1936 that Meccano offered a specific car construction kit. This initially comprised a chassis on which three different coachwork options were available, and was followed by a line of larger scale models. Märklin, the oldest of the clockwork train makers, also offered a car construction kit (in separate chassis form), on which six different vehicles – from a tanker to a monoposto racing car – could be built.

Mysto Manufacturing Co. was another US firm early on the scene. Their Mysto Erector was similar to Meccano in concept, and from 1915 included Gilbert clockwork cars. The company later became A. C. Gilbert & Co.

QUALITY TOO

The 'Rolls-Royce' of all construction kits was, undoubtedly, Ranlite. Strictly speaking, it was not a metal toy and does not belong under this heading, but it was an integral part of the kit scene of the early 1930s and is best considered in this context.

Initially at least three cars were offered by Automobiles (Geographical) Ltd of Halifax, the proprietors of Ranlite. Two were saloons – an Austin and a Singer – and the third was the record-breaker Golden Arrow. The cars boasted metal chassis (or base plates) and, in the case of the saloons, metal wings too, but the bodies were moulded in bakelite. For attention to detail, however, they were unsurpassed at the time, complete with opening doors and sun roof where applicable, realistically moulded upholstery, and wheels that steered. Such excellence, however, did not come cheap. The two saloons were priced at 35s. (£1.75) each, and the Golden Arrow was 27s. 6d. (£1.37½), and although these figures may seem paltry today, they should be measured against the 2d. or 3d. demanded for a small Dinky Toy die cast, the 10 cents required for an American cheap cast-iron type, or the 3s. or 4s. which would buy a large tin-plate motor car.

Suffice to say that only the children of the rich enjoyed the Ranlite – the firm were a latter-day Georges Carette – and although there were one or two isolated imitators, none approached their standards. Production levels cannot have been high, and survivors are rare and highly sought after.

These pioneer kit firms (Ranlite also offered completely assembled examples) were, however, perhaps a portent for the future, and the final chapter of the book will examine the growth of construction kits world-wide.

THE LARGER THEY ARE . . . THE HARDER THEY FALL

The inter-war years were not, however, without their casualties. Quite apart from the effects of political pressures in the Germany of the 1930s, the entire world suffered from the 1929 collapse of the American stock market – the infamous 'Wall Street crash' – and that event was followed by several years of stultifying economic depression.

In America alone, three thousand banks went to the wall directly or indirectly as a result of the 'crash', and everywhere respected names – particularly in the automobile world – foundered. The toymakers emerged remarkably unscathed, but with some notable exceptions.

Ignaz Bing, one of the founders of the firm bearing his name, died in 1919, and the company was thereafter endowed with a 'new broom' philosophy with the accession of Stephan Bing, which coincided with a period of great expansion. History has shown, however, that when manufacturing firms set up their own sales organisations and 'holding companies' not directly concerned in the manufacturing processes, they have frequently come 'unstuck'.

The most notable example in Britain was, perhaps, that of the Bean car. Basically a good vehicle, its sponsors lumbered themselves (and it) with a top heavy (and administratively expensive) selling organisation grandiosely titled The British Motor Trading Corporation. Not until it had divested itself of this millstone did Bean become even moderately successful.

As we have seen, the miniature automobile world often echoed that of its larger, full-size cousins, and it was the establishment of Concentra, Bing's own selling organisation, and over-expansion – with stock rooms and sample rooms becoming established throughout the world – which contributed to their downfall.

Any organisation which is geared to an ever-rising sales graph – as Bing had become – is bound to run into trouble once the graph levels out. From ten thousand workers in 1920 (more than one-third of whom were employed in making toys), Bing grew and diversified. By the late 1920s Concentra were handling sales of a variety of products totalling some 27 million Marks but the company lacked direction. Plummetting sales following the Wall Street crash left the company with acute cash-flow problems, over-capacity and high overheads – exactly the problems which faced the real-life automobile producers – and the only solution was to appoint a Receiver. Stephan Bing departed to concentrate on Trix and, although tin-plate toys continued to be produced until 1932 during the receivership, they were but a shadow of those produced in the company's heyday.

As in the case of Carette, Karl Bub stepped in to pick up the pieces when production finally halted, and some of Bing's more popular lines were continued under Bub's aegis. In 1933, during the changeover period, the Bing and Bub trademarks were side by side on some toys, but the Bing name soon disappeared. Bub themselves continued to flourish and eventually survived the war as well, despite Allied bombing of the factory.

TAKEOVERS AND AMALGAMATIONS

Other companies faced with financial difficulties managed to overcome their problems by amalgamating with a stronger competitor. Typical of these was the London firm of Brimtoy Ltd, who in 1932, at the height of the Depression, threw in their lot with A. W. Wells, an Islington toolmaker who had commenced tin-plate toy manufacture in 1919. He moved his company to Walthamstow in 1924 and was successful in securing a very valuable toy contract with the Woolworth store chain. By the end of the 1920s Wells were producing cars, fire engines and aeroplanes in tin plate, and a series of most attractive commercial vehicles lithographed in the liveries of real companies. These included a charming 'B.P. Motor Spirit' lorry, which reflects very closely the Caledon original in B.P.'s fleet, and delivery vans in the liveries of Carter Paterson and Express Transport.

These helped to establish Wells as the principal maker of cheap, lithographed tin toys in Britain from the early 1930s (as Wells-Brimtoy) until the late 1950s. The company were also intensely patriotic, and their double-decker London buses – made in various sizes and qualities – often carried slogans like 'Thanks for Buying British'.

LONDON GENERAL

The London bus was, in fact, a favourite theme for tin-plate producers everywhere, and the familiar red livery of the London General Omnibus Company – 'General' – was to be found on examples from Märklin, Günthermann, Distler, Tipp, and Bing of Germany (among others), Burnett and Minerva (Britain), Rico (Spain) and French makers not renowned for such lack of chauvinism.

Rossignol also certainly built buses, but they were uncompromising representations of the Schneider and De Dion Bouton single-decker, rear-platformed Paris buses of fond memory. There were, of course, many others, but limitations of space dictate the extent to which they can be discussed here.

We have mentioned Minerva, and this obscure but attractive maker crops up again with a Sentinel steam lorry and a truck, both beautifully and

34

authentically liveried in colours familiar on vehicles in the fleet of J. Lyons & Co. Ltd of Cadby Hall until relatively recent years.

IT PAYS TO ADVERTISE

The use of toys to publicise a company unconnected with the toy industry (unlike Wells-Brimtoy who used the advertisement panels of their buses to advertise their products) is not unusual, and was developed to the full by the die-cast manufacturers. In the tin-plate era, however, it took various forms.

It is not generally known that during or shortly after the First World War the giant Metal Box Company also entered the tin-toy field, and it seems likely that some at least of their offerings were in the form of decorated containers for confectionery and biscuits. This idea was not new, as some very crude car containers by Huntley & Palmer date from the turn of the century, but it was popularised during the 1920s and 1930s. These gift packs were sold by Huntley & Palmer's biscuits, Macfarlane Lang, John Hill & Son (biscuitmakers of Ashton-under-Lyme), Gray Dunn & Co., Crawfords, Mackintosh's Toffees, and many others. While their attribution is not always known, certainly the limousine tin offered by A. W. Dunmore & Sons (biscuits) in 1923 was made by Barringer Wallis & Manners Ltd, a firm of decorated tin makers which was later absorbed into the Metal Box Company.

Other containers were variously offered as double-decker buses, steam lorries, railway locomotives (Issmayer of Germany did one of these for Stöllwerck chocolate) and gipsy caravans, but one of the most attractive was the red, folding-head, two-door coupé from Crawford's Cream Crackers in the early 1930s, complete with lithographed flat-capped driver smoking the inevitable (1930s) cigarette. In America the theme was pursued by Victory with glass automobile containers for sweets.

STEEL TOYS

These are not strictly tin plate, but we have touched upon the makers of steel toys, and as the method of construction is more akin to tin plate than to die cast it is more appropriate to consider them here. Generally, they enjoyed greatest currency as a group in the United States, but there were notable exceptions elsewhere, some of which we shall examine.

Probably the most famous of the American steel toys was the range offered under the Buddy-L trademark and made by the Moline Pressed Steel Co. of East Moline, Illinois. The first of these appeared in 1922 and the name Buddy-L was reputedly derived from that of Arthur B. Lundahl, son of the owner of the company, for whom the first toys were made (shades of Hornby and his children). Thereafter the company became renowned for a range of trucks and other robust toys of generally indestructible 'child-proof' quality, similar to those offered by the Murray Ohio Mfg Co. under the Steelcraft label. Pride of the latter's line was a sturdy tank truck (tanker) modelled on the real-life G.M.C., which even boasted the G.M.C. radiator badge. Steelcraft had a marketing arrangement with the giant mail order firm Sears, Roebuck in which their toys were sold by Sears under the name 'Boycraft'. This avoided unpleasantness with their other smaller wholesale and retail outlets who had to sell the same toys at a higher price than Sears.

Chein, although mainly tin plate, in the US, also offered steel toys under the Hercules trademark; Mysto, Gilbert and Structo have already received mention, and there were a number of others including Corcoran, Sturditoy, Kelmet and Keystone, which are included in the appropriate appendix to this book.

Friction propulsion was a popular method employed by American toymakers between the wars – indeed, had first been used there by Clark as early as 1904. Other makers to favour this cheap method were Dayton, Schieble, Turner and Republic, the latter being made by Republic Tool Products Company of Dayton, Ohio. These people, in common with Dayton, had concluded an arrangement with the United Cigar Store chain whereby trade certificates could be redeemed for toy cars and other goods. Green Shield and S. & H. Pink Stamps are not such a new idea.

By far the most popular medium in the United States would, however, appear to have been cast iron (which will be dealt with in the die-cast section of the book), but steel construction was also favoured by Lines Brothers in England. It is hardly surprising that they used steel since many of their toys were of the large, pull-along type, and pedal cars, tricycles and other toys-to-ride were also made. Lines Brothers should not be confused with the older firm of G. & J. Lines, although there was a family connection. Walter, William and Arthur Lines broke away from the family firm (of which their father was part-owner) and founded their partnership in 1919. Their trade-mark of an 'L' within a triangle was intended to symbolise their triumvirate, and in 1924 they moved from London to a new factory in Merton. Further expansion ensued in 1931 when one of the finest and oldest-established toy and model shops in Britain – and perhaps the world – was taken over.

MINIC AND TRI-ANG

The 'Toy Store' in Regent Street became an even greater Mecca for children, and the range was gradually expanded to include toys of steel, steel and wood, and eventually tin plate. Their Minic range of tin-plate vehicles was issued under the parent Tri-ang trademark, and over a period of years achieved astonishing variety.

The Minic vehicles were all clockwork powered (although some steam lorries and vans with long-running clockwork were also produced) and were, perhaps, the first clockwork tin-plate toys to appear in which a serious attempt had been made to achieve correct scale. All were rubber-tyred, and such was the diversity of the eventual output that a whole book is warranted (and, indeed, has been written, see appropriate appendices) to give the collection the merit it deserves. Considering the small scale to which they produced and the difficult medium – tin-plate – of which they were constructed, they came closer to being (like their die-cast rivals) scale models than most of their predecessors. Details included petrol tanks on running boards, steering wheels, and trailer caravans with opening doors, complete with wooden furniture within!

NAMING THE MAKE

It was also possible to identify the full-size 'prototypes' (a term used by collectors to denote the original source of a toy or model), and the range included not only the Ford Model 'Y' saloon but also more exotic makes like Rolls-Royce, Daimler, Bentley and Vauxhall. The last is interesting in that it represents virtually the only known example of a 1930s Vauxhall in either tin plate or die cast ever to have been made. Pre-war Minics, like most of their die-cast contemporaries, wore white rubber tyres, but those models (like the Vauxhall) which continued in the post-war period changed to black rubber. The presence of white rubber tyres is, however, not necessarily proof of the age of a toy, since tyres, like other accessories, are removable, perish with age, and may have been changed during the life of the toy.

VARIATIONS ON A THEME

Reference to specific marques or 'prototypes' being recognisably portrayed in toys and models does bring us, however, to the question of thematic collections. The first thing a potential collector will realise is that the scope is vast, and it is the easiest thing in the world to 'get on one's horse and ride off in all directions'.

Many collectors prefer, therefore, to concentrate upon a single theme – either the complete range offered by one toymaker, or perhaps all the representations of a single make of 'prototype', e.g. Vauxhall. Even though Vauxhalls have been poorly represented as a marque, the Minic range alone provided quite a number of variations in body style, colour and accessories (loudspeaker on the roof of the police car, and so on).

Other marques have enjoyed much better coverage – particularly Ford Model 'T', Austin Seven, Rolls-Royce and the more sporting types – and the collector must decide whether his collection will concentrate solely upon, say, tin-plate examples of Ford cars, or range over the whole gamut of die-cast, cast-iron, wood, composition, rubber, plaster, steel, plastic and other options which have at one time or another been available. Other collectors will decide to base their collections on military themes, or fire-fighting perhaps – an enormous number of toymakers have portrayed fire engines, pumpers and escapes and the Lee and Larned self-propelled fire engine offered in the US by Stevens and Brown before the turn of the century was probably the first working model 'automobile', in the widest sense, ever made.

ACCESSORIES

It should not be overlooked, in this context, that many toymakers offered accessories with their vehicles, ranging from the two-car garage – a most attractive tin-plate example came from Oro-Werke Neil, Blechschmidt and Müller of Brandenburg under the Orobr trademark, together with two tin-plate cars loosely modelled on the Delaunay-Belleville – to the commercial garage complete with petrol pumps offered by Tri-ang.

As we have seen, Jouets de Paris (JEP) set new standards in France, but arguably the most famous tin toy ever made was the P2 racing 'Voiture de Course' Alfa Romeo produced in the mid-to-late 1920s by Compagnie Industrielle du Jouet (C.I.J.). Of amazingly complete specification, far more accurately to scale than most of its contemporaries and painted, among other colours, in the racing blue of France, it included wheels that steered, correct Alfa Romeo badges, a radiator grill of fine mesh, detailed suspension, filler caps that really opened, knock-on wheels and a louvred bonnet correct and faithful to the original upon which it was based.

QUAI DE JAVEL IN MINIATURE

It was this company which, in 1936, took over what was, and still is, a unique venture in toymaking – the toys of André Citroën. Citroën, flamboyant womaniser and gambler though he was, nevertheless built up the most successful automobile company in France between the wars. With a background of gear-cutting for other manufacturers (similar to the David Brown firm in Britain), he commenced manufacture of his own cars in 1919 and, mainly on borrowed money, beat his archrival Louis Renault (who had never borrowed a *sou*) into second place in the production race.

Citroën cars were advertised from illuminated signs on the Eiffel Tower – a thorn in Renault's side – and as an *entrepreneur* André proved himself virtually unbeatable. In 1923 he launched Les Jouets Citroën, his own toy factory located at Briare, the purpose of which was twofold.

PAPA, MAMA . . . ET CITROËN

Based on the premise that today's children are tomorrow's Citroën buyers, the main *raison d'être* of the toy firm was to publicise the products of the parent company. Citroën told his agents 'the child is our future client. His first three words must be Papa, Mama and . . . Citroën.' He may have been joking, but his second object – to make available to children a toy 'just like Daddy's' which reflected the quality of his main product – was sound, and the brilliance of his thinking is reflected in the fact that no less than 15,000 Jouets Citroën were sold in the first year, rising to 274,000 in 1933 at the height of the Depression.

A companion range of die-cast Miniature Toys was introduced in 1928; the production of these toys rose from 5,200 to 576,000 in 1933. Since the 10CV Torpedo of the first 1923 trial run was quickly supplemented by a sedanca de ville, a truck, saloon, coupé, car chassis and also a range of pedal cars, the company quickly captured for itself a broad slice of the toy market.

In 1934, from a brand new factory, Citroën's revolutionary and stunning 'traction avant' 7CV full-size car was introduced, but the building of the new factory and re-tooling necessary, coupled with Citroën's personal excesses, severely strained the company's finances. He was forced to sell out to Michelin interests in 1935, and his toy company went to C.I.J. the following year. No company was better qualified to carry on, however, and Jouets Citroën continued to be made by C.I.J. up until the outbreak of the Second World War. Post-war production passed to J.R.D. but only a few toy Citroën T45 trucks were made before production ceased.

TWO WHEELERS TOO

One aspect of road vehicle toys not covered so far, and more rarely encountered than cars or commercials, is the motorcycle. Many attractive versions of both solo and combination machines were, however, offered by a variety of makers, including Tipp, Paya, Lehmann, Arnold, Einfalt, W.K., Kico (Kienberger), Gely (Levy), C.K.O. (Kellermann) and G & K (Gundka), a few of which were made before the First World War.

Tipp were particularly active in this field, their late-1930s example boasting not only a passenger in the sidecar and a pillion passenger behind the rider, but a concealed battery supplying power to an electric headlamp. Motive power was, however, by clockwork. Gundka went one better and included a dog which scampered along beside the front wheel!

INTERNATIONALISM

Manufacturers catering for an international market made various attempts to suit their toys to the countries in which they were intended to sell, and this leads to certain amusing discrepancies which are worth noting. Distler's 'General' omnibus of 1925 – a very early roofed-in version, albeit with outside staircase and exposed driving position – advertises Crystal Palace Fireworks on its side, but renders the spelling as Cristal Palace Fireworks!

Obviously Germanic saloons and racing cars – some of them loosely modelled on Mercedes – nevertheless have 'Dunlop' lithographed prominently on their tyres, and while it seems doubtful whether any motorcycle was ever fitted with 935 × 135 tyres, Tipp depict one of their models thus endowed! However, such idiosyncrasies add to, rather than detract from, the charm of the toys.

SAWDUST AND GLUE

As in the case of some of the Lines Brothers' vehicles, manufacturers did not confine themselves to one medium, frequently combining wood and steel; and in Germany particularly, composition mouldings were frequently incorporated with tin-plate toys, increasingly towards the end of the 1930s.

Prominent in this field were Hausser who, together with Tipp, Lineol and Hess, dominated the military vehicle toy market from about 1936 onwards. Accessories, and even parts of complete vehicles (the sidecar and passenger of a motorcycle combination, for example) were often composition mouldings, and Hausser's patent substance – a mixture of sawdust and glue called Elastolin – had in fact been in use since 1926. Many of the toy soldiers – drivers, passengers and those on foot – which were sold with their toys were made of Elastolin. Complete vehicles of composition materials will, however, be dealt with in the final chapter of the book.

NOVELTY TOYS

Although novelty toys were not quite as common between the wars, a number of ingenious and amusing examples were made, and some of these

40

are worthy of mention. Eberl, another victim of the 'Wall Street crash' with Bing and Ives of the USA, made an attractive open tourer (*c*. 1925) which not only drove forward by clockwork, but also contrived to roll over! It achieved this manoeuvre by means of small activated outrigger wheels beneath the running boards, and curved hood supports which acted as 'anti-roll' bars for want of a better description.

Moko's saloon, dating from the same period, featured not only forward and reverse gears, but also (beneath an opening bonnet) a six-cylinder engine, with pistons exposed and undulating on a crank, each ringing a small bell at its extremity! Another, unknown, manufacturer endowed his saloon (like Tipp's motorcycle) with electrically operated headlights, whilst Günthermann offered a luxury cabriolet in either two- or four-door versions, with a canvas roof which could be rolled back either partly or completely. Opening doors and boot completed the refinement.

During the 1930s Louis Marx offered a simple crawler tractor with continuous tracked wheels which possessed an uncanny ability to surmount obstacles, pursuing its erratic, unmanned course in the manner of a latter-day Moon buggy. Schuco developed a line of cars with an ingenious mechanism which prevented the car from tumbling over the edge when it reached the end of a table or surface. Instead, the car was diverted to right or left and swerved through 180° by means of a small, centrally placed wheel located underneath the car at the front. Another small German coupé called the 'Six' (an allusion to the number of variations activating the steering mechanism rather than the number of cylinders!) was depicted as a 'runaway' pursuing an erratic course despite the efforts of its operator.

Distler's 'Fares Please' bus appeared conventional at first glance, but when propelled forward by clockwork, its conductor 'walked' up and down the gangway on the open upper deck, turning as he did so to collect fares from the tin-plate passengers seated on either side.

Martin of France (under the aegis of Bonnet et Cie) also produced a complicated and fascinating dump truck. Not only did the mechanism propel it forwards, but also stopped it, tipped the body sideways to discharge its load (of whatever the child had placed in it), righted it, and recommenced its journey.

Kellermann applied their ingenuity during the 1930s to a motorcycle with rider and pillion passenger. Two outrigged small wheels amidships would ground alternately to prevent it falling over if the machine leaned to either side. The front wheel could be steered to left or right, and when the machine turned the pillion passenger turned and leaned inwards, returning to the upright position when the front wheel straightened.

These versatile examples will serve to show the uninitiated the enormous scope which even simple clockwork mechanisms gave to the more inventive manufacturers, and there were many more variations, too numerous to detail here. Understandably, most of these toys and their mechanisms were covered by patents to prevent infringement by unscrupulous companies, and many of the toys carried confirmation of these.

PATENT PROTECTION

On German toys, the letters 'DRP' indicated that a full German patent had been granted – Deutsches Reich Patent – while D.R.G.M. indicated a second grade or utility patent having a limited life of three (or occasionally six) years. (Germany's detractors during the late 1930s were heard to insist, however, that the initials stood for Damned Rotten German Muck!)

U.S.P. on an American toy indicated 'United States Patent' (usually followed by the patent number itself); 'dep' on German toys was a shortened version of 'deponiert', meaning that the patent had been deposited (mainly used in and around Nuremberg); while the addition of the word 'ang', meaning 'angemeldet', was the equivalent of the British 'patent applied for'.

Lehmann in particular – possibly because of their addiction to novelty toys during the early Edwardian period – invariably indicated their patent numbers and trademark prominently on the toy, even going to the lengths of gumming an additional paper sticker to it listing overseas patent numbers if the toy was to be sold in any great number abroad.

As these patents, in whatever country they are granted, are normally issued numerically, they can be found in the appropriate patent office, and thus dated accurately. Beware, however, that you do not assume that the date of a patent is also the date of a toy. Patents granted might not necessarily be incorporated into a retailed toy for some years, and others, covering ideas with many applications, might continue to be incorporated into different toys for many years. Lehmann, for example, were still quoting patents granted in 1903 in the lithography of some of their toys well into the 1920s or even later.

DATING AND IDENTIFICATION

Dating a toy is a difficult business, and like the whole science of toy collecting it is still very much an area in which even the experts are learning something new every day. As manufacturers, jobbers, wholesalers, mail-order and retail catalogues gradually come to light in attics and jumble sales, a picture is being built up; but in the case of toys which remained in production for many years – sometimes under different managements – the nuances of colour and detail difference are only slowly being detected and noted.

In the case of manufacturers whose toys are totally unknown – the German maker W.K. is an example, where only recently has attribution to Wilhelm Krauss been confirmed – the problem becomes even more difficult, particularly as some toys tend to look older than they really are.

Most manufacturers either trademarked their wares or – as in the case of Carette – they were so distinctive as to be unmistakable in their attribution, and a glossary of the trademarks of the major tin-plate makers will be found in Appendix VI. Included among these are some important, but less illustrious, houses with which we have not yet dealt, and since the vehicles made by any of them would form a worthy addition to any collection, a note of some of them would, perhaps, be helpful.

WINNERS AND 'ALSO RANS'

Karl Arnold of Nuremberg commenced relatively late (in 1906) and initially their toys were characterised by a built-in sparking flint for which the firm held a patent. Apart from a range of fire engines, few road vehicles were made, and most of these were not destined to appear until after the Second World War.

Louis Marx are notable for the fact that, alone among the major American and German producers, they established an entirely separate British factory at Dudley in the industrial Midlands. Marx came to prominence during the 1920s with a wide range and a successfully aggressive marketing policy which enabled them to buy up many of their smaller competitors (including the old-established New York company Strauss, Man & Co.). By the 1930s, Marx was the largest toymaker in the world, but not necessarily the best. Most of the Marx range was sold through F. W. Woolworth stores, the American Kresge chain and by mail order, and tended to be rather crude both in subject matter and execution. The parent factory concentrated on vehicles based on those of government agencies – police cars, fire engines, fire chief's cars, trucks of the US Medical Corps, ambulances, Volunteer Fire Department Emergency Squad, and so on – in addition to the usual range of limousines, coupés and commercial vehicles.

COMIC-STRIP CHARACTERS

Both the saloon and coupé of the mid-1930s were loosely modelled on the Pierce-Arrow car, but there was another drophead which took its inspiration from the front-wheel drive Cord of 1937, and a wide range of novelty types, many of them deriving from comic-strip characters like Popeye or other children's favourites of radio and films – Charlie McCarthy, Mortimer Snerd, the Disney Dipsy Car with Donald Duck, and a 'Dick Tracy' Police Station in tin plate together with three Dick Tracy Squad Cars.

Another Dick Tracy squad car was friction-driven, and mounted with a machine-gun and electrically operated flashing roof light. The machine-gun emitted sparks (similar to the system employed so much earlier by Arnold) and this theme was repeated in the 'Gang Busters' and 'G-Man Pursuit Car'. A wide range of motorcycles of the 'carrier delivery', solo and combination type was also offered.

MILITARY INFLUENCE

Military vehicles also played their part, the 'Doughboy' featuring a crude representation of a First World War tank – the Mark V. From a hatch at the rear the 'Doughboy' would emerge, point his rifle at the sky, and then retreat to safety once more. This tank, which was also issued by a French manufacturer, compares unfavourably with a much more realistic, yet toylike, offering from Whitanco (Whiteley Tansley & Co. of Liverpool). This featured realistic moving tracks with tensioning adjustments, rivet details, fake gun barrels and a hatch at the rear which opened to facilitate inspection of the 'motor'.

These toys first appeared towards the end of the 1920s or around 1930 when a revival in interest in the First World War was stimulated by the very successful films *All Quiet on the Western Front* and *Hell's Angels*. Similarly, during the Italian campaign in Abyssinia in the mid-1930s Marx produced a copy of the lightweight tank used in the desert by the Italian forces. Strangely, this was available on the British market, although made by the American parent company, and this would appear to have been the case with other items in the Marx line despite the activity of the Dudley subsidiary.

Joustra of Strasbourg-Neudorf was founded in 1935 by Guillaume Marx, but was in no way related to the American company of the same name. A German by birth, Marx had left for France in 1933, having previously been a director of Bing. A range of mechanical tin-plate toys were made until 1939 and then again, very successfully, after 1945.

I.N.G.A.P. of Padua, in Italy, were also newcomers after the First World War. Founded by Giovanni Casale, Pietrol Zihelli, Tullio and Anselmo Anselmi and Giorgio Zattla in 1919, the firm took its initials from 'Industria Nazionale Giocattoli Automatici Padova', and at first made only toy trains. By 1934, tanks similar to the Marx offering (and with the sparking flint mechanism in the gun barrel) were also made, a reflection also, perhaps, of the growing influence of the Fascist military dictatorship of Mussolini in Italy during this period. Until the Second World War cars were also made, and as with Marx, some toys incorporated themes derived from comic strips and other children's characters, e.g. Felix the Cat and Pinocchio. By the 1930s the company was controlled by Mario Benacchio, and by the time he died in 1936 I.N.G.A.P. had become the largest Italian maker of tin-plate toys. Thereafter, and without his guidance, the company declined. From a peak in the 1930s when about six hundred staff were employed, the firm's influence lessened, and they were eventually taken over in 1972 by Eurotoys.

Another Italian firm worthy of note during this period, but whose products are rarely found outside their native country, was Cardini. Established in Omegna in 1922, it flourished briefly for six years making a quality range of trains, ships, cars and aeroplanes, and standardising on a coil-spring mechanism. The trademark of two outspread wings pierced vertically by an arrow was always stamped in relief into the tin plate rather than litho-graphed thereon, and the toys are, therefore, easy to identify. With such a short production run, dating is not a problem either, for Cardini ceased production in 1928 for unknown reasons – the Wall Street crash was still a year ahead.

Heinrich Wimmer, whose trademark of HWN was incorporated with two faces which we would now call 'Smileys', started his Nuremberg company in the same year that Cardini bowed out, buying his clockwork mechanisms from Buhler, an old-established (1860) company who had moved from Triberg in the Black Forest to Nuremberg in 1924 (Schuco, incidentally, also relied on Buhler clockwork until 1934).

THEN TRAINS ONLY

Wimmer built a range of aeroplanes, cars and mechanical animals until the Second World War, concentrating on train sets after 1945. This rational-isation into trains in the post-war period was a feature of many of the firms previously active in the general toy field, and was mainly brought about as a result of the inroads into the ordinary tin-plate market made by cheap die-cast and plastic vehicles in the 1930s and 1940s. We will be looking at these in the final chapter. During the 1930s, most of the original tin-plate manufacturers remained faithful to this medium and, allowing for the effects of the Depression and the persecution of the Jews in Germany, there were remarkably few casualties of note other than Bing and Ives.

Hans Eberl offered relatively few automobile toys during the 1920s and, like Bing, the company was liquidated, in 1929. This is an intriguing late offering dating from about 1925 and of rather crude construction. It is ingenious, however, in that the mechanism not only propels the car forward, but tips it sideways. The hoops supporting the hood enable it to roll over through 360°, eventually righting itself. E, U.

A well-preserved example of Lines Bros double-decked omnibus dating from about 1930. They reissued this wooden toy about three years later in six-wheeler form and with the staircase inside, but still with open driver's cab. Both 'ran' on Route 123, and both were in 'General' livery. E, U.

Peter Doll's company always concentrated on steam engines and steam-driven toys in addition to novelty and tin-plate toys, and this large (50 cm long) steam-driven four-seater open tourer is typical. The hinged bonnet gives access to a horizontal boiler with wick burner; three of the side doors are hinged for opening, and the car boasts rubber tyres, operational clutch and wheel steering. It dates from the 1920s, during which period a steam-powered chain-driven lorry was also offered. S, R.

Bing expanded rapidly during the 1920s, and one of their most popular range of toy vehicles was that based on the Model 'T' Ford. This example is the typical open four-seater 'Tin Lizzie' and it was also made as a two-seater coupé, truck, open two-seater and charabanc. Unlike Henry Ford, however, Gebrüder Bing did not make their fortunes. The 'Wall Street crash' of 1929 brought receivership and eventual closure, although Karl Bub took over some designs. M, U.

This London taxi and four-seater open tourer are both mid-1930s tin plates from the Tri-ang Minic range, and both have in common a can of Shell petrol on the nearside running board. Actually, this was an anachronism dating from the 1920s (when petrol was not so readily available at the pump) but toys (and children) are conservative. We are not told how the passenger could have opened his door without dislodging the can! M, U. (Museum of Childhood)

Another smoker's companion dating from the mid-1930s. The roof of the car lifts up to disclose a cigarette box which dispenses its contents from beneath the running board as the car is rolled forward. Antique shops and curio stalls are a good hunting-ground for these items, but country house sales and provincial auctions can also be rewarding. M, U. (Peter Richley Collection)

Meccano offered three separate sets of car construction kits during the 1930s, and Kit No. 1 offered various permutations on the same chassis, of which this is one. Loosely based on the SS1, M.G. and Singer sports models of the period, it came in a number of colour options, this example being in scarlet and cream. E, I. (Tiatsa Toy Museum)

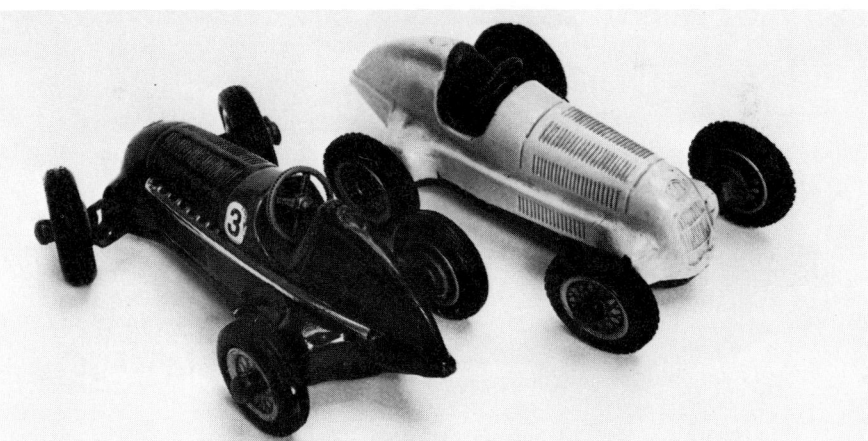

Two Schuco racing cars labelled a Mercedes (in white) and an Alfa Romeo (red). Both, in fact, are identical pressings but for the three-pointed star on the grill of the Mercedes! Clockwork, they are interesting in having shaft and bevel drive to both rear wheels. M, U. (Museum of Childhood)

C.I.J. (Compagnie Industrielle du Jouet) took over Jouets Citroën in 1936 after Citroën himself was forced to sell his automobile business to the Michelin tyre family. This is a rare Jouets Renault toy by C.I.J. based on the Renault two-seater Vivasport coupé, and reflects the American styling influence prevalent in France at the time. The headlights are battery-operated, the wheels steer and clockwork drives the rear wheels. S, R.

Always better known for their trains, Märklin nevertheless produced some very attractive motor vehicles during the Edwardian period and between the wars. When the construction kit craze (sparked off by Meccano) swept Europe they offered this smart two-door coupé (No. 1101 in their range), together with a racing car, truck, tanker, Pullman limousine and armoured car, all on the same chassis kit (which was sold separately). A smaller scale Mercedes was also offered. M, R.

A detailed and amusing motorcycle and sidecar combination by Tipp & Co. of Nuremberg, dating from the early 1930s. Not only has the machine a rider and pillion passenger, but also a *kleine baub* in the sidecar. Clockwork powered, the body of the motorcycle also concealed a battery which powered the electric front headlamp. S, R.

This excellent and rare tin-plate Sentinel six-wheeled steamer, despite its English lettering, is of German origin, and was made by Tipp & Co. around 1930. It is 53 cm long, is chocolate brown and cream (authentic vintage colouring) and clockwork drives the centre axle. S, R.

This Karl Bub novelty toy originally appeared in the 1911 Georges Carette catalogue, and the radiator bears a strong resemblance to that of the Carette limousine. The car, when wound, follows an erratic pattern, turning to left and right, stopping and then reversing, and all apparently controlled by the driver's hand on the gear lever. This example was produced *c.*1920 after Karl Bub had acquired the Carette pressings. S, R. (Museum of Childhood)

Toy cars were often sold with matching accessories, and typical is this garage by Lehmann, housing (in unlikely proximity) a saloon and a racing car by the same maker. Oro-Werke offered a similar twin garage under their Orobr label, together with two Delaunay-Belleville type automobiles, and Rossignol of Paris provided their dual cowl Delage with a handsome motor house. The German Post Office van is also by Lehmann, and all date from about 1930. S, R.

Lehmann were to the fore with novelty toys during the Edwardian period, and some of them were quite fiendish in their complexity. While the driver of this hansom unconcernedly steers a rather drunken route, the two Auto Sisters try in vain to beat off the stray dog with their umbrellas. M, R. (Museum of Childhood)

Following in the traditions of Doll et Cie are the products of Mamod. Stationary engines and traction engines with spirit or solid fuel-fired boilers are the most popular items in the range, but this steam-driven two-seater car in heavy gauge metal, but with plastic seats, is well made and attractive. M, C.

Although uncompromisingly a tin-plate toy, there is yet something almost real about this Günthermann tram. It is this rather enigmatic charm, never intended by the makers (or was it?), that attracts collectors of tin-plate vehicles today, particularly to earlier examples like this one, which dates from about 1930. S, R. (Tiatsa Toy Museum)

The Meccano constructor kit with some alternative parts. Three separate construction kits were offered by the company from the mid-1930s. The sports car shown here is heavy influenced by M.G., SS1 and other popular marques of the day. M, U. (Museum of Childhood)

It is interesting to compare this Russian-made modern die-cast toy of a four-seater Russo-Baltique with the scratch-built model made by Gerald Wingrove for *Automobile Quarterly* magazine. Although, like Lesney, the Russians incorporate a certain amount of plastic for the hood, upholstery and other detail, the general quality is very good, and the toy recognisably based on the car in the Moscow Polytechnic Museum. M, U. (Tiatsa Toy Museum)

Three of the most popular models in the Lesney range, the Model 'T' Ford (in this case endowed with a tanker body) and two variations of the Talbot van. In offering reproductions of real-life advertisements on their vans, Lesney are but repeating the lead given by the tin-plate lithographers of the 1920s and by Dinky Toys with their 28 series (and later vans). M, C.

One of the most popular of Günthermann's toy car series was that devoted to Gordon Bennett racing cars. Issued in various sizes and forms and sometimes with both driver and mechanic, they were modelled quite closely on the Wolseley racing car driven by the Hon. C. S. Rolls in the 1904 Gordon Bennett Trials. Racing cars are, understandably, a recurring theme with toymakers. M, I.

The inimitable Georges Carette limousine in all its glory. This version has both head-lamps and sidelamps, bevelled glass windows, forward and reverse gears and opening rear doors. It dates from c.1910 and in this condition would command several thousand pounds at auction. This example is in the Victoria & Albert Museum. S, I.

In stark contrast to the Georges Carette, yet amusing and evocative, is this American friction-driven toy – probaby by Dayton of Ohio. The friction drive is transmitted by the fifth wheel located between, and slightly forward of, the rear wheels. It is very typical of the rather crude, cheaper American toys and is made of a heavier gauge metal than its European counterparts; c.1910. E. R.

This very early horsedrawn bus in tin plate was made by Neil, Blechschmidt and Muller, the proprietors of Oro-Werke. Toys were produced under the Oro and Orobr labels until about 1922, at their factory at Brandenburg. S, R. (Tiatsa Toy Museum)

Decorated tin containers date back to the late nineteenth century, and vehicles have been a popular theme. Not only did large firms like Metal Box Company make these (they also briefly entered the toy business in the early 1920s), but they were also made by such established toymakers as Chad Valley. They probably supplied this splendid 1930s coupé, complete with electric headlights and turning wheels, to William Crawford, the biscuit makers. M, R.

This very attractive ambulance was made by H. Fischer of Nuremberg around 1918, and is very similar to limousine versions from the same maker. Later types included a windscreen and headlamps. The roof rack with its curly forward ends is a typical Fischer feature. M, R.

A traditional red double-decker bus by Lehmann dating from either just before or just after the First World War. Lehmann differed from their contemporaries in that they did not identify the bus as being from the 'General' fleet of the London General Omnibus Co.; neither did they lithograph English advertisements on the side panels. As a result, some of the neo-realism is perhaps lost. M, R. (Museum of Childhood)

A clockwork open tourer by Bing of Nuremberg. Similar types were made both before and after the First World War, and this one probably dates from about 1920. It is interesting in that the pressing for this toy is virtually identical to that used in Britain by Brimtoy, and bearing a 'British made' slogan. S, R.

This large tin-plate refreshment bar truck is post-war and probably made by Mettoy,
although no trademark is readily discernible. The proprietor's name 'A. Snack'
emblazoned on the cab door is typical of the atrocious puns beloved by toymakers
and, presumably, children too. E. R. (Tiatsa Toy Museum)

Representatives of two famous British toy firms comprise this line up. The trolley-
bus is post-war from Wells-Brimtoy and advertises the company in the appropriate
panels along its sides. Wheels are of plastic. The tanker and the open touring car
are, however, both from Minic, with that unmistakable Shell petrol can on the
running board. The tourer is pre-war (note the white rubber tyres) but was also
made after 1945. M, U (trolley bus); E, U (rest).

Günthermann's trams were very effective visually, and this example – lithographed in red with yellow lining, with glazed windows, hinged power pick-up arm and axle-activated bell – dates from the 1920s. It is driven by clockwork to the rear wheels. E, R.

Post- and pre-war Chad Valley buses side by side together with a just post-war lorry from Tri-ang. All reflect the fact that few new designs of full-size vehicles, let alone toys, had yet reached the market, and in any event many popular toys continued to follow traditional designs long after their full-sized prototypes had been updated. S, U (all).

An example of how toys can be updated over a period, this Karl Bub limousine is based on the 1910 design, but has a glazed windscreen fitted, together with scuttle-mounted sidelights, and there is provision above the front wings for headlamps (now missing). In another version, the driver's door is cut away; *c*. 1918/20. E, R.

Another novelty tin, this time containing breakfast cereal and dating from the late 1920s. The roof of the vehicle hinges back to give access to the interior. Many of these tins were made by Metal Box Company and similar firms, but toy firms also made them for biscuit and sweet manufacturers. E, R. (Peter Richley Collection)

Citroën's epic trans-Sahara Expedition of 1922 with Citroën-Kegresse half-track vehicles was enough to inspire the heart of any boy, and this robust and faithful toy version (the original of which is now in the Musée de l'Automobile Française) echoes the auxiliary radiators and caterpillar tracks of the originals (one of which is preserved at Compiegne). S, R.

One of the most popular styles of traditional fire engine, this example was made by Wells in the late 1930s but was still in production (with more modern headgear for the firemen) in 1948. Similar examples were made by Distler, Bub and Tipp throughout the 1930s. M, U. (Museum of Childhood)

A large and substantial looking late 1920s limousine by Distler of Nuremberg. Attractively lithographed in primrose and black with navy and orange lining, it boasts electric headlamps (a feature found on Tipp and other makers' toys), illuminated tail-lamp and registration number, and Continental Balloon Cord tyres. A tin-plate driver pilots the equipage, which is powered by clockwork. M, R.

This tin-plate limousine dates from the mid-1920s and is probably by Bing. It is interesting, however, in that it features a small radiator mascot in the shape of Felix the Cat. Felix was as popular in the 1920s as Mickey Mouse was in the 1930s, and several novelty toy cars featured him as the driver. It is unusual to see this representation, however, which echoed the mascots in his image which were available for full-size vehicles. S, R.

With its coal-scuttle bonnet and rear-mounted radiator (see the filler cap just in front of the windscreen), this J.E.P. toy saloon could not be mistaken for anything but a Renault. Painted olive green with black wings and chassis, it boasts headlamps, spotlight and klaxon horn, and is remarkably true to life. It somehow lacks the charm and colour of its more toy-like competitors, however; *c*.1928. S, R.

How Günthermann saw the London double decker in about 1930. This tin-plate clockwork toy carries advertisements for Ford cars and is interesting in that, like the Lines Bros offering, it has an outside staircase but covered-in upper deck. In the late 1920s many L.G.O.C. 'K' type buses were updated in this way and fitted with pneumatic tyres. Six-wheelers were a short-lived fashion of the early 1930s. S, R.

This 1930s motor caravan from Lines Bros 'Tri-ang' toys incorporates a tin-plate radiator, sheet steel chassis and plywood body construction. It is complete down to opening windows, caravan furniture and an iron stove! A battery clipped under the chassis operated a small electric bulb in the caravan. E, U.

Two similar open tourers from German makers, and both dating from *c.* 1912/14. That on the left is unmarked but possibly by Günthermann, while the brown car on the right, with its driver hunched purposefully over the wheel, is by Bing. The similarity of the pressing of the Bing car to that of the Brimtoy version is intriguing. Brimtoy also made (or offered) a similar version with mudguards (like this Bing) and clockwork propulsion. M, R (both).

This Dennis van is interesting in that it illustrated, both on the roof and along its sides, all the many varieties of games made by the manufacturer, Chad Valley. The roof would appear to be removable, so possibly a selection of games was contained inside. Chad Valley made a number of 'container' toys for biscuit makers and confectioners during the 1930s. S, R.

Possibly one of the most sought-after toys of all time is the classic P2 Alfa Romeo 'Voiture de Course' issued by C.I.J. *c.*1928/9. Offered with authentic markings, suspension, fuel and radiator filler caps and correct in virtually every detail, it is to be found in red, blue and cream, and possibly other colours. M, I.

This Günthermann open tourer was made both before and after the First World War, and this is probably a post-war example. It is unusual, however, in having a fixed 'starting handle' similar in appearance to that found on Hess toys. In this case, however, it is presumably used to activate the clockwork mechanism. S, R.

The Parisian firm of J.E.P. started life as La Société Industrielle de Ferblanterie (S.I.F.) in 1899, taking the title *Jouets de Paris* in 1928. From the latter date they commenced making a line of tin-plate automobiles which paid closer attention not only to scale, but also to authentic detail. It was thus possible to identify the actual marque portrayed, as with this Delage. S, R.

The luxury of this mid-1930s Günthermann folding-head cabriolet, with its fabric hood, trunk and liveried chauffeur, contrasts with the little Hess coupé de ville of some ten years earlier. While the Günthermann is clockwork powered, the Hess relies upon a heavy flywheel drive activated by the 'starting handle' – a Hess trademark. S, R.

Racing and record-breaking cars have always been firm favourites both with toy and model makers. This Sunbeam record-breaker was made by the American Kingsbury company (previously Wilkins up to 1920), well known for their 'sealed patent clock-work motors'. It is based on the Land Speed Record car in which H. O. D. Segrave set up a new world record of 203.7 m.p.h. in 1927. They made a similar toy in 1928 of Sir Malcolm Campbell's Napier Campbell Special (Bluebird) which raised the record to 206.96 m.p.h. in that year. M, I. (Museum of Childhood)

Two excellent examples of British tin-plate toys dating from the very early 1930s. Both are made by Wells and, characteristically, look older than they are. The BP Motor Spirit lorry is authentically liveried in red and green with gold lettering, while the Carter Paterson van is dark green. S, R (lorry) (both).

The 1930s and 1920s are graphically represented in these two excellent, large, tin-plate toys. The saloon on the left is apparently British made, but is similar to some Tipp and Distler designs of the late 1930s. Possibly it is by Mettoy, who had Tipp connections, but it appears better made and better proportioned than most of their range. The Lehmann 'Gala' taxi dates from about 1930 and is, unusually, blue and cream. Most examples are red and cream, and it is the differences in detail, like this, which add value. S, U (both).

It is interesting to compare the late 1930s saloon offered by Tipp with that from Mettoy in England. Mettoy were formed in Britain by the Ullmann family who had formerly controlled Tipp until the rise of Nazism in Germany. Being Jewish, they were forced to leave Germany, but they obviously brought some ideas with them! S, U.

During the 1920s the 5CV Citroën became a legend for robust construction and reliability. When André Citroën introduced his Jouets André Citroën in 1923, therefore, it is perhaps only natural that his Briare toy factory should include the 5CV in its range. Well made and true-to-life, these Citroën toys were immensely popular. Hand-enamelled in primrose (Citroën Citron) with black trim, the interior is scarlet. Sadly, the spare wheel and windshield are missing on this example, but note the front-axle detail. E, R.

Three splendid mid-to-late 1920s buses from Bing, Distler and Rossignol of France. The two German types are based on the traditional London double decker, complete with advertisements (note the mis-spelling of Cristal Palace!). Rossignol, however, concentrated on the typical De Dion Bouton Paris bus with its rear entrance and mounting platform – a familiar sight on Paris streets until quite recently. S, R (all).

CHAPTER THREE

WAR AND PEACE

THE OLD ORDER CHANGETH

Despite the widespread effect of the Second World War and the devastation in Britain, continental Europe and Japan caused by bombing (in Japan's case, including the dropping of atom bombs on Hiroshima and Nagasaki), toy production did not cease altogether, although many of the larger factories were given over to production of war materials.

On 21 August 1944, however, Hitler issued an order banning the production of further toys in Germany, and by that time the quality of toys produced elsewhere had deteriorated steadily as materials became more scarce. Many firms turned once again to the discarded products of the canning industry for their tin plate, and many a child was disillusioned to find, on removing the base plate of a favourite toy, the words 'Cadbury's Bournville Cocoa' or some similar legend lithographed on the inner surfaces.

Understandably, there was a growing tendency during the war years for toy vehicles to reflect the preoccupation of the populace with matters military, and army trucks, staff cars and tanks displaced lorries, sports cars and bright red fire engines in the affections of the young.

As time went on more toys were made of wood, composition or bakelite, and it was not until after 1946 and the ending of the war in the Pacific that new tin toys began to appear in the shops in any appreciable quantity.

NUREMBERG DEVASTATED

Bearing in mind the extent to which Germany had been battered during the conflict – Nuremberg was the subject of a heavy air raid on 2 January 1945, and heavy shelling and bombing in the final attack by American forces in April 1945 virtually obliterated the old city – it is surprising how quickly many of the older pre-war companies rebuilt their factories and re-established themselves.

Of this old guard, Tipp & Co. (under German reparations) reverted to the control of the Ullmann family who, nevertheless, continued their Mettoy interests in Britain; Distler continued under the direction of Volk; Doll came under the control of Fleischmann (who had taken over many of their designs in 1938); and Einfalt (Technofix) gradually turned over to production of plastic toys.

Günthermann maintained an independent existence in Nuremberg until 1965, having rebuilt their factory for the last time in 1951, but in the former year Leonhard Günthermann, who had been in control since 1919, retired and the firm passed to Siemens, the electrical giant.

Hausser, like Einfalt, switched to plastic in 1955, as did Höfler (newcomers in 1938), and Lehmann was revived by the Richter family and established in 1951 (for the first time) in Nuremberg. Levy's old company, the Nuremberg Tin Toys Company, lasted until 1971; Lineol found themselves in the Eastern Zone of Germany; and Kindler & Briel of Böblingen (established in 1865) co-operated with Distler but gradually switched to plastic.

Georg Fischer lasted only until 1958, having supervised the rebuilding of the Trix factory which had been taken over by Volk, but which was destined to pass to Gama in 1971. Gama was the trade name adopted in 1924 by Mangold, whose first toys appeared in Fürth in 1882. Their post-war Cadillac and Opel, introduced during the mid-1950s, were outstanding examples of the art of the tin toy.

AMERICAN INFLUENCE IN GERMANY

In the early post-war years, Mangold also produced a number of Schuco designs under licence – including their novelty 'roll-over' car – and the American influence was strong, largely because most of the German toymakers were located in what had become the 'American Zone' of the armies of occupation.

Duplex (a new name) offered a rendering of the Oldsmobile, Tipp a Chrysler 'Dream Car' and a Hudson saloon, while Günthermann preferred the Ford Custom. Toys made in Nuremberg and district at this time often bore the legend 'Made in the American (or US) Zone of Germany' – later, simply 'Made in West Germany'. Arnold produced various versions of a graffiti-covered 'Jalopy' loosely modelled on a Ford Model 'A' with rumble seat (the graffiti being in Americanese), and, seemingly alone during this period, CKO (Kellermann) built an articulated lorry based on the then-current Hanomag, and an open tourer and saloon of distinctly European lines.

Schuco, in business since 1912, now entered what many consider to be their best period. In addition to a range of conventional clockwork vehicles, all extremely well finished and lithographed, they also offered an increased variety of toys incorporating unusual mechanical actions, but of sufficiently 'childproof' sturdiness to ensure long life on the nursery floor.

FIRST OF THE ROMANTICS

Of particular interest was their series of 'Oldtimers', a most attractively and authentically produced collection of toy replica veteran cars of mainly European origin (but including a Model 'T' Ford), which they continued to make until the 1960s. It is interesting, because it catered for the growing demand for nostalgic toy vehicles which received great impetus following the British film *Genevieve* released in 1953.

Schuco too, however, succumbed to the American influence, producing a remarkably true-to-life replica of the 1958 Packard Hawk which incorporated all the exaggerated tailfins and chromework of the American 'gingerbread' era epitomised by the Gama Cadillac. Although they were among the best of the post-war tin-plate manufacturers, Schuco gradually concentrated on other toys after the end of the 1950s, and thereafter fewer toy cars or other vehicles were produced.

In France, JEP were still in business, but their Renault Nervasport racing car and Delahaye saloon were a pale shadow of the beautiful cars made at the end of the 1920s, and Rossignol's Laffly fire engine and American-style 'turret-top' coupé (bearing a passing resemblance to Marx's coupé of the same era) were of much better quality.

AMERICA'S POST-WAR PROGRAMME

Peacetime found Marx in a strong position. Based in the USA, they had suffered no bombing and less shortages than their European contemporaries, and their post-war range made up in exuberance and numbers what it lacked in quality and taste. Their police-siren car, crude in the extreme, but robust, was powered by a strong clockwork motor and was endowed with a convincing replica of the authentic American police siren, which must have endeared it to its recipients.

Kingsbury, famous for their sealed clockwork motors in America before the war, and eventual owners of Structo, had, however, taken the decision to cease toy manufacture during the war, and emerged in 1946 as makers of machine tools only. Another well-known American maker, Lionel (albeit concentrating upon train sets), found the post-war going difficult and was eventually absorbed into Metal Product Corporation – a division of the giant US firm General Mills – and other old-established companies also began to find the market for tin-plate toys, if not in decline, certainly contracting.

It was also shifting, and gradually more and more firms succumbed to the cheap competition from an area which, in pre-war times, had been but a mild irritation; from a country apparently of second-rate copiers and plagiarists; from that group of islands which had survived two atomic bombs and retained its Emperor and its culture; from Japan.

AMERICAN INFLUENCE IN JAPAN

Just as Marshall Aid to Germany assisted in the post-war economic miracle of that country, so the American presence in Japan must have materially accelerated the Japanese recovery, and in no area was this recovery more dramatic than in the tin-plate toy industry. Many of the early toys made from 1946 onwards were, of course, very crude and insubstantial, and examples bearing the legend 'Made in Occupied Japan' are now valued more for their rarity than for their aesthetic merit.

As we have seen, however, the Japanese had always possessed the potential necessary to produce really good quality tin-plate vehicles, and as they gradually found their industrial feet, so their confidence and their ability matured. Prominent among these early Japanese post-war producers were Alps Shoji Ltd (1948), Asahi (1950) and Haji (1951), but possibly it was Bandai (1950) who typified the best of the Japanese 'invaders' who now appeared in the American and European markets.

Like the German manufacturers, and understandably in view of the strong military US presence in Japan, Bandai's earlier cars were strongly American in flavour. Their 1957 Ford Fairlane, however, was successful in capturing not only the likeness of the prototype, but, like Gama, the atmosphere of America of the 1950s, and the toy is as well made as any from Europe during the same period.

Bandai were joined by T.N. (Nomura Toys of Tokyo), T.P.S. (Toyplay, Tokyo), Rabbit (Usagiya), Taiyo (Tokyo) and a host of others, most of which upheld totally the traditions of the earlier German manufacturers. T.N. (and M.T.) would appear to have been wholesalers or marketing agents rather than actual manufacturers, in which role they continued the traditions of the Kohnstam family. However, although all these Japanese toys were available on the European market, it is clear from their styling and presentation that they were primarily intended for the US market.

CHEAP LABOUR

It was certainly in America that the Japanese toys first began to have an impact, and eventually even such giants as Marx were unable to compete. Japanese labour costs were, of course, very much lower than those of either America or Europe at this time, and it is this factor more than any other which gave the Japanese the edge over their competitors.

Marx switched to plastic-moulded toys in common with many of the remaining German manufacturers, but even the more cheaply produced plastic versions found difficulty in competing with a flood of small, cheap, Japanese 'penny' toys – the direct descendants of those originally offered by Distler, Meier and others. Of course, they no longer cost only 1d., but taking inflation into account, their position in the market was the same as that enjoyed by their pre-war counterparts.

JOUSTRA SURVIVE BUT COPY JAPAN

The Japanese did not totally dominate the post-war scene, however. In France, Joustra, the company started by Guillaume Marx, was destined to flourish and, alone of its American and European competitors, to concentrate – and continue concentrating – in tin-plate products. Eventually, many of the better German designs – including the Gama Cadillac already mentioned – were taken over by Joustra, and their 25th Anniversary catalogue issued in 1959 included some Japanese designs.

Joustra had refined the art of tin-plate toymaking by combining ultra-thin gauge tin plate allied to sophisticated tooling, permitting greater detail than was ever previously possible. We found that Bandai's 1957 Ford Fairlane appeared in the Joustra range, and with this paradox comes the realisation that the wheel has turned full circle. Where the Japanese were once content to copy Europe, the reverse is now the case.

Not all the American manufacturers made the immediate transition to plastic, however. Several preferred the rearguard action of establishing plants in Hong Kong to take advantage of the cheaper manufacturing costs prevalent there. Among the old-established makers, Buddy-L took this step, and when the Japanese themselves forsook the tin-plate market for plastic, Hong Kong also became the centre for many European and American producers of plastic toys.

TIN-PLATE REARGUARD IN BRITAIN

In Britain, the surviving toymakers – and there had never been very many – found things difficult. Supplies of tin plate were scarce, competition from Japan and Germany was fierce, plastic was becoming a force to be reckoned with and, in the austerity of post-war Stafford Cripps' economy, there was little money for luxuries.

Wells-Brimtoy were in the vanguard of British tin-plate manufacturers during this period. Their toys were more cheaply and crudely produced (some with plastic wheels) than heretofore, but were still bravely emblazoned with patriotic exhortations to 'Buy British'. A new factory, founded at Holyhead, concentrated on toys, while the parent company diversified into clocks and household goods, but the end of the 1950s saw the closure of this venture. A. W. Wells died in 1965 (he was 77) and the company was taken over by C. M. T. Wells Kelo Ltd.

MECCANO AND DINKY TOYS TAKEN OVER

Lines Brothers, who between the wars had enjoyed such a strong position with their wide range of toys, also ran into a series of financial difficulties after the war. Their primary tin-plate division, Minic, was eventually forced to adopt plastic, but a new Lines factory was built at Merthyr Tydfil in Wales, and in 1964 the group acquired Meccano Ltd of Liverpool. It thus took under its wing Meccano, the die-cast Dinky Toys (of which we shall hear more in the last chapter) and Hornby trains, and an empire which extended to New Zealand, Canada, Australia, South Africa, India and elsewhere. There is an old saying about those who ride two horses. It seems likely that in trying to 'hedge their bets', Lines bit off more than they could usefully chew, and the whole company became too large and unwieldy. The successive dramas which beset the company are, however, more a matter for the die-cast enthusiast, since Dinky Toys became virtually the only viable division in the group, and even these eventually succumbed in the 1980s.

Mettoy were a different story. While the Ullmann family's resurrection of Tipp in Germany met with rather less success (eventually closing down in 1971), Mettoy continued the pre-war tin-plate range in Britain until about 1954, when they successfully made the transition to die-cast toys with the Corgi range (and smaller Husky die casts sold through Woolworth's). These will be dealt with in the next chapter, but it is significant that the successful Kohnstam marketing interests were also able to make the move from tin-plate to die-cast toys about the same time, although they allied themselves to the completely new Lesney company.

A few forlorn tin-plate newcomers such as Camtoy appeared briefly on the scene, but thirty years after the war there were no serious producers of tin-plate in Britain, and even the sacrosanct world of the model train had been invaded by the plastic-moulding machines.

PLASTIC TAKES OVER

Apart from questions of economics and availability of raw materials, however, there were other considerations which accelerated the change in buying habits during the post-war period. Plastics were becoming more popular in the household goods market, and this led to a wider acceptance of plastic goods generally. As far as toys were concerned, the stronger plastic proved just as durable, if not more so, than tin plate; it did not rust when left out all night in the garden; it did not develop jagged edges; and it was easier to clean.

Although it excelled in making tin-plate toys, Japan therefore also eventually diverted its resources to cheap plastic ones, and for some years tin toys declined in the market to the point where their presence in the toyshops was the exception rather than the rule. In recent years, however, they have re-appeared, albeit (with the exception of Joustra) from an entirely new area.

'IRON CURTAIN' INVASION

An easing of relations between East and West since the days of the Berlin Airlift and the 'cold war' has witnessed an increase in trade with the Soviet bloc countries, and with this increase has come the need for the Russians and their satellites to generate more foreign currency. By heavily subsidising such products as motor cars, this has been partly achieved, and the Russian Moskvitch, the Czech Skoda and the Polish Lada are now commonplace on the roads of Western Europe.

One suspects that toys from the Eastern bloc are also similarly subsidised. Certainly they are cheaper to buy, and the tin-plate versions have arrived here at a time when collector interest (as well as that of the nursery) in tin plate has reached a high level.

Tin-plate toys are not a new industry in Russia, Hungary, Czechoslovakia or Poland; it is simply that until relatively recently there was no serious market for them outside their native countries. Although naïve, and in some cases crude, most of them are surprisingly good; some Czech examples are even fitted with a three-speed gearbox! However other Eastern countries are relatively new entrants to the world of heavy industry and of these both Korea and Taiwan are now supplying tin-plate toys to the West. How long it will be before these protagonists follow their predecessors and move into plastic totally one cannot say, but one thing now seems clear: the tin-plate toy, once in danger of extinction, is alive and well and seemingly here to stay. Admittedly its sponsors and espousers move from continent to continent every ten years or so, and its followers include more adults in some cases than children.

But with the benefit of hindsight, who is to say that we are not ripe for a revival of the 'penny' toy (costing its 1980s equivalent of that devalued coin, to be sure), or even a European renaissance of wholesale tin-plate toy manufacture?

It is interesting to compare this modern Russian tin-plate motorcycle combination with the pre-war version by Tipp. Russian vehicles generally tend to be old-fashioned in appearance, and this motorcycle has girder forks of a type abandoned in Britain in 1946! It is colourful and well made, however, and the standard of lithography is high. These Russian toys can be purchased very cheaply and would make a good thematic collection. M, U.

This post-war tin-plate taxi by Ne-kur bears a passing resemblance to the Chinese ambulance, but was actually purchased in Istanbul! The ideologies of China and Turkey being singularly opposed, it seems unlikely that there is a connection, but it is not certain that Ne-kur is an indigenous Turkish maker. M, U. (Tiatsa Toy Museum)

Although one does not associate the Iron Curtain countries with toys, there is no doubt that in both the die-cast and tin-plate field the quality to be found there is as good as any in Western Europe or America. This Russian-made Zim saloon is complete and authentic down to the radiator badge, grill and glass headlamp lenses. A 'remote control' toy, it comes with hand trigger and 'Bowden' cable, and dates from about 1954. M, U. (Tiatsa Toy Museum)

Despite their archaic appearance, both these Chad Valley toys in tin plate are post-Second World War. The Green Line bus follows the pattern of similar buses made pre-war but has lithographed windows showing passengers, while the pre-war version had simple cut-out windows. There is a family resemblance in the saloon to the coupé made for William Crawford in the 1930s. S, R.

This Wells' tin-plate van probably dates from just after the Second World War, although similar types were offered in the 1930s. The small plastic truck was made in Japan and is interesting in that it was produced at a time when tin plate was fighting a losing battle against plastic. It compromises, having a plastic cab but tin-plate grill and tilt. E, U.

Just how good Japanese tin-plate toys could be is amply illustrated in this scarlet and black Buick sedan with cream wheels which dates not from the 1920s but from the 1960s. It would not be out of place alongside Bing, Distler and Tipp, and was made by Ichiko. It is not difficult to see how Japan 'took over' from Germany, America and Britain from the 1950s onwards. M, R. (Tiatsa Toy Museum)

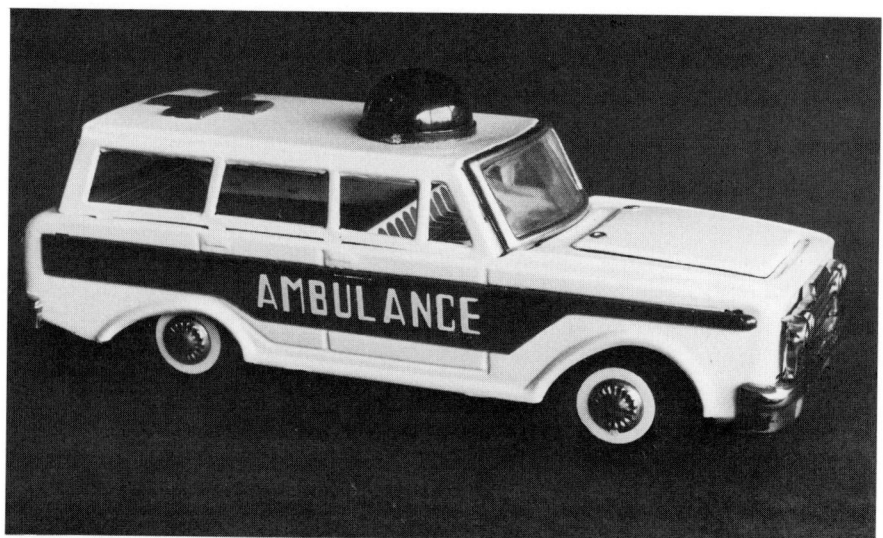

If this Chinese-made tin-plate ambulance (complete with flashing blue light) is not readily identifiable, it is probably because it is based on an indigenous Chinese prototype. China does not export her cars, and apart from the odd Embassy car they are rarely seen outside China. China is becoming a prominent tin toy manufacturer, and exporter, however, and while lacking in finesse the quality of the toys is good. M, U. (Tiatsa Toy Museum)

Before the Second World War very few versions of Hitler's 'strength through joy' car – the Volkswagen – appeared in tin plate, but this deficiency has been more than corrected since 1945. These two versions (one a patrol car of the German Automobile Club – A.D.A.C.) are in tin plate but with plastic seats and hoods and perspex windscreens. Of West German origin, they are unmarked and are just two VWs from a myriad of designs produced by different manufacturers. M, U. (Tiatsa Toy Museum)

Friction drive, originally espoused by the American manufacturers in the first forty years of this century, was taken up with enthusiasm by the Japanese in the 1950s and 1960s. This very passable Jaguar Fire Chief's car (missing its roof light) is friction powered and was made by Ichiko of Japan. Now it is the turn of China and Korea to adopt the simple and cheap friction transmissions. D, U.

R.S.A. was the trademark of the Spanish Rico concern, and their logo was an attractive bi-plane. This simple tin-plate petrol tanker is probably just post-Second World War, although most toys of this type remained in production for several years and look of early vintage. S, R. (Tiatsa Toy Museum)

The rise in the demand for 'nostalgic' or 'romantic' toys and models after the Second World War gave rise to a spate of representations of veteran and vintage cars which, to the uninitiated, might appear at first to be of real age. These three cheap Japanese veteran and vintage 'penny toys' date from the 1950s, are of poor quality tin plate with crude lithography, and yet ... are amusing. D, U. (Tiatsa Toy Museum)

Times were as difficult in post-war Japan as they were in Europe, and this red Chrysler made in virtually one simple pressing is scarcely elegant. It is stamped 'Made in Occupied Japan', which probably accounts for the American theme, and is interesting on this count. It was not long, however, before the Japanese toy market found its feet. E, U.

Cab meets cab. The realistically styled Ford Fairlane 'Yellow Cab' on the left dates from the late 1950s and was made by Toymaster of Japan, while the S.E.A.T. (Spanish Fiat) is, predictably, by Rico. It is a feature of post-war tin-plate cars that in many cases the manufacturers have made a real effort to identify with the actual marque on which the toy is based. Before the war this was not usually the case, the exceptions being J.E.P., Jouets Citroën and the Fords made by Bing, among others. M, U. (Tiatsa Toy Museum)

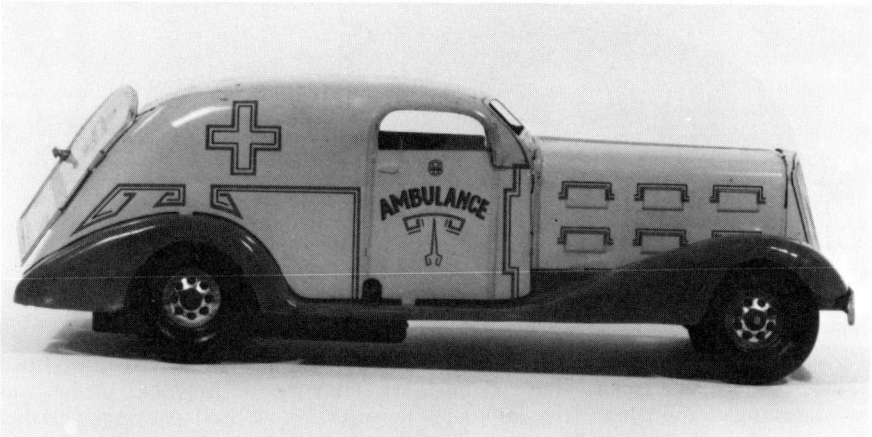

There is something rather brash and American in most of the toys made by Louis Marx – particularly those dating from the 1930s, 1940s and 1950s. This rather crude ambulance is nevertheless purposeful-looking, and utilises many of the pressings from their Siren Police Car (of which the same could be said). Of 1930s' design, both were made in the 1940s and 1950s. S, U.

Three cheap tin-plate toys from the 'Gingerbread era' of portholes and mouth-organ grilles – the 1950s. The 'Highway Patrol' on the left, despite its American looks and odd number plate, is English-made and is interesting in that a real photograph is lithographed 'at the wheel'. The Chrysler 'Town & Country' in the centre is, predictably, from Marx, while the two-door Sixmobile on the right is German from Gescha. S, U.

Few sports car manufacturers have inspired more toy replicas of their models than Ferrari, in tin-plate (as with these examples by Bandai of Japan and Jouet Mont Blanc of France), die cast and plastic. Bearing in mind that these two models were both made at opposite ends of the earth, the similarity in size, construction and quality is quite remarkable. S, U (Tiatsa Toy Museum)

The modern equivalent of the 'penny toy' has persisted and will probably continue to do so as a traditional 'stocking filler'. These cheap cars, both by F.A.B. of Germany and both in the same series, are, for all their simplicity, robust and adequately detailed. The clockwork mechanism is wound by a key inserted in the hole in the front wing. M, U. (Tiatsa Toy Museum)

CHAPTER FOUR

NOT ALWAYS FOR CHILDREN

CAST IN THE MOULD

It might be thought from the information provided in the three preceding chapters that the die-cast toy and the other alternatives to tin plate were all a result of the upheaval caused by the Second World War and, therefore, of relatively recent origin. Nothing could be further from the case.

The mechanical toy soldiers fashioned by Hautsch in 1660 were of silver, and their basic forms were probably created in a mould. Certainly the toy soldiers made by William Britain from the turn of the last century onwards were moulded in lead, and the concept of the moulded toy is as ancient and acceptable as is the tradition of tin plate.

Since we are here concerned with motor vehicles, it is probably true to say that the cast toy got off to a later start than its tin-plate cousin, but certainly William Britain was offering a cast steamroller as early as 1908, and the American Dowst company produced a limousine in 1911. This same early toy was later (*c.* 1917) made by Cosmo, albeit with non-moving wheels, by which time Dowst had produced a Model 'T' Ford tourer (1914), a Model 'T' truck (1917), and these were supplemented by another cast Ford tourer with solid disc wheels early in the 1920s.

The Dowst company is important, since it was later to play a decisive role in the American die-cast toy industry, but there may well have been earlier cast American vehicles. Because they were more popular with the American market, however, and to avoid confusion, it is probably as well to differentiate at this stage between the various forms in which toys were cast.

METHODS OF MANUFACTURE

Cheapest and most common was the 'slush' cast toy. Usually made of soft metal – lead was a favourite – it was formed in an inverted female mould, into which the molten metal was poured. Before the metal had cooled totally, the mould was righted, allowing the still-molten centre to be poured off and leaving the cooled outer metal 'shell' intact. These 'slush' moulded toys can be recognised by their uneven interior finish and the roughly elliptical hole in their base. Wheels were added in subsequent operation processes.

Cast-iron toys were usually cast in a sand mould in two separate halves, subsequently joined together. These joins are usually imperfect and, in the case of a vehicle, usually dissect the unit vertically and longitudinally.

Die-cast toys, in which the detail and finish are invariably superior to those produced by other methods, are, as the name implies, cast in a die under pressure or, in the case of more modern toys, by the application of centrifugal force to ensure an even distribution of the metal.

US CAST IRON

It is difficult to say who produced the earliest cast toy vehicle, but the two largest cast-iron toymakers were early in the field and, strange to say, never trademarked a single toy! They were Dent Hardware and A. C. Williams, but other US makers included Stevens Bros; Champion; Freidag Manufacturing Co. of Freeport, Illinois; Kilgore; Shimer; Vindex; Arcade; Kenton; Hubley; and Grey Iron Casting Co. (unusual in that their Model 'T' Ford has been in continuous production since the 1920s, but as a decoration rather than a toy).

Prominent in the slush cast field were Kansas Toy & Novelty Co., but Metal Cast Products Co. of New York offered stock moulds to many small, anonymous companies for hand slush casting. As a result, many vehicles from different manufacturers are similar if not identical. This makes attribution difficult.

The cast-iron theme was carried to a reasonable level of sophistication in the 1930s, with Williams offering a cast-iron chassis on which could be fitted four interchangeable bodies; and Kilgore's model of the Graham Straight Eight Supercharged was comparable in quality with the die-cast type offered by Tootsietoy.

TOOTSIETOY AND DINKY TOYS

It was in the field of pressure die casting, however, that the greatest strides were made and the highest quality achieved, and the first significant company to adopt this method of production was Tootsietoy. Predictably, it was Dowst, whose Model 'T' Ford toys had appeared so early on the scene, who produced the Tootsietoy range.

According to the authoritative modeller's journal *C.A.R.S.* (published in Millbrae, California), the name 'Tootsietoy' derives from the pet name 'Tootsie' given originally to Ted Dowst's daughter (shades of Buddy-L), and initially the Model 'T' Ford was incorporated in the Tootsietoy range introduced in the mid-1920s.

From 1932 Tootsietoy used a zinc-based alloy of high quality, and appear to have succeeded in achieving quality control at an early date, unlike their later (and nearest) rivals, Dinky Toys. Dinky Toys made their appearance in Britain in 1934, having been first announced in the December 1933 issue of *The Meccano Magazine*, the semi-house magazine of Frank Hornby's group of companies. They had, in fact, appeared in a photograph printed some months earlier as accessories in a railway layout, and this was their prime purpose at this early stage. They were not initially called Dinky Toys, but Hornby 'Modelled Miniatures', and the Dinky appellation followed in April 1934. The first issue, numbered 22a–22f, consisted of a sports car, a sports coupé, a motor truck, a delivery van, a tractor and a military tank.

From this beginning a vast range of scale-model vehicles – many of them identifiable with actual full-size makes and types – issued from the factory. A French factory was also established, making a different range for the continental market, a few examples of which were available in Britain. From being accessories enhancing and lending reality to model and toy train layouts, the Dinky Toy became one of the most popular small toys available in the 1930s. There is insufficient space to describe all the variations in this book, but readers are recommended to refer to Cecil Gibson's *History of British Dinky Toys* (Model Aeronautical Press, and reissued in 1973 by Mikansue), the lavish tome recently published by New Cavendish Books and written by Mike and Sue Richardson on *Dinky Toys and Modelled Miniatures*, and *Histoire des Dinky Toys Français* – Editions Adepte.

Tootsietoy and Dinky Toys dominated their respective sides of the Atlantic in the die-cast field before the war, but although the Dinky range was greater the quality tended to be variable. Dinky Toys were made of an alloy called Mazak, usually zinc or lead based, but of different composition from time to time. This resulted in varying degrees of stability in the make-up of the metal, and (particularly when a toy has been exposed to extremes of temperature) fatigue can manifest itself.

METAL FATIGUE

Metal fatigue normally takes the form of crazing and expansion of the metal, with distortion of the surfaces, resulting in an elongation of the toy which has often misled the uninitiated into thinking they have discovered a new, rare issue! Such problems were, of course, of little concern to the children for whom the toys were originally purchased, since a toy normally has only a limited useful life in the hands of a normal, healthy child.

It is, however, a problem which now faces collectors, and apart from the application of Araldite or some similar adhesive, there is little that can be done to save a toy so affected. There has long been a popular rumour that

Dinky Toys made during the early part of the war were susceptible to this fatigue, and that this was attributable to the lower grade alloys that the company was then forced to use. In fact, there appears to be little evidence for this, and fatigue appears in toys of various ages.

OTHERS TOO

It would be wrong to assume, however, that Tootsietoy and Dinky Toys were alone in producing good quality scale-model toy vehicles during this period, and in America both Hubley (who had been important early cast-iron manufacturers) and Barclay Manufacturing Co. switched to die casting with success, and vied with Manoil (futuristic vehicles rather crudely interpreted), Erie and Savoye.

Tootsietoys marketed through the Woolworth chain were renamed Playtoys, and the old-established firm of F. A. O. Schwartz marketed a 'Traffic Police' set comprising traffic signs, policemen and motor cars, the latter being supplied by Tootsietoy. By the end of the 1930s, the metal die-cast toy seemed set to sweep aside its older tin-plate competitors, and probably would have done had it not been for the war.

But other toy vehicles were also available, and if one ignores the rather crude two-dimensional (flat) cast vehicles offered by Hill in Britain, there was always the kit-built car. We have already examined the 'constructor' kits available, but there were also cheaper, and older, types employing a variety of materials, usually glued together with adhesive.

WOODEN KITS

Earliest of these was probably the Modlwood series issued in 1913 in the USA by Schoenhut, but various German, American and British companies offered similar kits from the 1920s to the 1940s. During the war, when metal toys became scarce, alternative materials came into their own, and typical of the kits offered during and after the war were Wilson lorries, the 4 mm and 8 mm scale brainchildren of the enigmatic D. Murray Wilson of Haywards Heath in Sussex, whose factory was at Bracknell in Berkshire.

Wilson's kits were mainly of wood, with plastic cabs and cardboard for mudguards and other details, and despite the limitations of these materials, were exceptionally good. Their counterparts in the United States were, perhaps, Miniature Trucks Co. of Benton Harbor, Michigan, who offered $\frac{1}{4}$ in. scale wooden kits, or Ace Products of Pasadena, California, who made $\frac{1}{2}$ in. scale kits in wood during the 1940s and 1950s.

Modelcraft Ltd of London SW1 took the post-war austerity era to its ultimate, however, with their 'Lineside Lorries' and 'Micromodels' series, in which the models were sold as printed coloured cut-outs on card, together with a detailed plan and elevation and assembly instructions. This theme was pursued much later by Riko (another company in which the Kohnstams had an interest), but although neither of these ventures made much impact, the Modelcraft plans were eventually to gain a new lease of life.

WARTIME NOSTALGIA CREATES A DEMAND

As the war years permitted nothing new in the way of automobiles or other vehicles (as one can gather from reading any of the then-current motor magazines), they were a time for looking back. In the dark days of the Blitz and Dunkirk, and while huddled in an Anderson shelter at the bottom of the garden, it was time for rose-coloured spectacles, and the seeds of the great post-war nostalgia boom were sown.

In the tin-plate world, Schuco were quick to cash in on this when peace returned, with their 'Oldtimers' range, and in America two companies stand out as being in the vanguard of both the post-war kit car 'explosion' and in the race to satisfy the demand for romantic or nostalgic models. Gowland and Gowland supplied their kits in plastic, and are generally considered to be the 'Daddy' of the plastic 'old car' kit makers. At least two dozen manufacturers are said to have cribbed their ideas from Gowland and Gowland models!

A. J. Koveleski's Hudson Miniatures, however, were $\frac{3}{4}$ in. scale antique automobiles built mainly from wood, although moulded plastic was adopted later, and a $\frac{3}{8}$ in. scale series was sold to Revell (another pioneer in plastic kits) to be sold on the British market. Fador Manufacturing of Elmira, New York, also offered their 'Smallster' models, and Mod-Ac of California included a representation of the '1877' Selden car in their range.

Aristo-Craft Distinctive Miniatures went one better, however, supplying battery-powered lamps for Hudson Miniatures in just the same way that scores of accessory manufacturers had supplied 'extras' for Henry Ford's Model 'T' during the 1920s. Altogether, more than seventy-five kits were offered in the United States between 1945 and 1953, and eventually the list of manufacturers included Renewal Products, Model Product Corporation, Testor Corporation, Plyro Plastics, C. J. Ulrich & Co. (metal kits intended as accessories for railway layouts), American Russkit (0.48 scale race track accessories), Austin-Kraft, Revell, and many more.

THE SLOT-CAR CRAZE

Coincidental with this interest in kits, however, and initially in the United States, there grew up in the 1950s another interest – slot-car racing. This reached its zenith in Britain about 1970/71, and was popularised during the 1960s by such firms as Scalextric. It was, somehow, an offshoot of both the toy and the model market, and was espoused as enthusiastically by adults as by children, although interest in America had waned by the mid-1960s.

This growing interest in toy and model cars – which before the war had been the province purely of children (and the occasional adult model railway enthusiast) – was probably stimulated in the first instance by the nostalgia created by the war, and the 'romantic' and 'nostalgic' kit cars which followed. It was no longer considered childish to 'play' with small motor cars, and slot-racing – the racing of model cars on a closed circuit with the car picking up its electrical power through a central slot in the track, and by means of which it was prevented from leaving the track on corners – spread like wildfire.

Certainly, slot-racing kits were bought for children as well, but clubs sprang up both in Britain and the United States for what had basically become a group participation sport – like ten-pin bowling. The art of making one's car go faster spawned fresh interest in the construction of scratch-built cars (home-constructed using some bought-in parts and some fabricated by the operator).

THE ADULT COLLECTOR

So now there was adult participation. I suppose it is true to say that, to an extent, there always had been, but interest until this time had been confined mainly to miniature engineering – steam-driven models and so on – and model railways. In 1964 and 1966 respectively, two books appeared, neither of which was to prove a definitive work, but they were both in the nature of a watershed in the history of toy and model cars.

The first was *Model Car Collecting* by F. Brian Jewell and the other was Cecil Gibson's *History of the British Dinky Toy*. These two titles brought together the nostalgia and history, and the acknowledgement of the collecting hobby as a respectable adult pursuit.

Gibson's book in particular was to become a mini-Bible on Dinky Toy matters for over two decades until the Richardson book appeared, and it gives us some insight into the subculture which exists in the world of model-vehicle collecting. From 1964 onwards, there has been an increasing interest in scale models, particularly in H0 (3.5 mm to the foot, or 1/87 scale), or 00 (the Dublo of railway modeller's fame) (4 mm to the foot or 1/76 scale). Not all makers are totally true to these scales, and most of the die-cast toys and white-metal models appear in 1/43 scale (although Dinky are often misquoted as 1/43, most of those produced up to 1963 were, in fact, 1/48).

But we are anticipating history. The rise and fall of slot-racing (actually very much still with us, but at nowhere near the level it enjoyed during the 1950s in the USA) was followed by a number of firms catering for the demand for white-metal scale models. It is probably largely due to the activity of Lesney Products, a post-war British firm, that this was so.

94

LESNEY AND MATCHBOX

It would be an over-simplification to say that Lesney took over where Dinky Toys and Tootsietoy left off, but suffice to say that whereas from the 1960s onwards Dinky Toys' position as market leaders declined, Lesney's (until relatively recently) increased. Whether this decline was due to the absorption of Meccano/Dinky into Lines Brothers, with all the financial disasters which ensued for that group, is not clear, but it is a fact.

Without doubt, Lesney introduced new standards of die casting into toymaking, and their early models (particularly those in the Matchbox – a trademark shared with J. Kohnstam Ltd who were bought by Lesney in 1959 – 'Models of Yesteryear' series) bridged the gap between true toy and model. The series was collected as enthusiastically by adults as by children, and became popular in the United States – more popular even than Tootsietoy, who were (and are) still a force to be reckoned with and a part of the Strombecker Corporation. Barclay, too, were strong competition for Dinky, and Hubley (now part of Gabriel Industries Inc.) proved to be an important and innovative post-war producer in the USA.

Corgi, too, were important (and still are) in the post-war die-cast scene. Successfully making the transition from tin plate, Mettoy (later Mettoy-Playcraft), however, never quite equalled Dinky Toys in popularity or in the attractiveness of their models, although its slogan 'the ones with windows' underlined an important innovation which helped their sales. Smaller 'Husky' models were sold through the Woolworth chain (in which Corgis were not initially available) and the company is still thriving.

PLAGIARISM OF MODELCRAFT

Lesney, however, had shown the way and it was not long before some small independent die-cast manufacturers (often one-man businesses) were setting up to supply white-metal kits to adult collectors. Many of these found the plan drawings of the long-defunct Modelcraft firm (thousands of which had been distributed when the company had been active) invaluable, and copied them without shame over and over again!

Because of this, white-metal kits from different producers are often difficult to attribute without close examination, while others covering the same subject vary greatly in quality, all of which makes for confusion. The one fact which becomes apparent, however, from any study such as this is that toy and model making is a financially hazardous and capricious business, in which extinction rather than survival is the rule rather than the exception. Possibly this stems from an apparent ineptitude on the part of manufacturers when it comes to choosing suitable subjects for models. A die-cast or plastic Austin Ten of the 1930s would evoke much more nostalgia, and probably sell better, than a Bugatti or an Hispano-Suiza, yet none has been offered!

CO-OPERATION OR COPYCAT?

Yet, while the companies themselves may cease to exist – Dinky Toys are no longer with us and Lesney is a shadow of its former self – quite often the dies and moulds themselves live on under new sponsors, and the same designs keep popping up forlornly, like a drowning man. Sometimes the reappearance or continuation of a model is the result of a licensing agreement with another country – thus we find Dinky Toys made in India still available, and also to be found there under the near-anagram Nicky Toys!

Similarly, in the plastic world, 1/87 scale plastic kits given away by Jet Petroleum at one time are found to have originated from Harbutt's plasticine. They, in turn, acquired the design from an obscure (and defunct) antipodean producer, 'R.L.' of Australia.

But the ramifications of these licensing agreements, sales of dies and moulds, bankruptcies, changes of company name and downright plagiarisms are difficult to sort out, and there are few who have managed to unravel the machinations of those companies who have at some time or another produced toys in association with the London Die Casting Company.

Not all the companies involved have any direct connection with each other, but many have shared designs with one firm who have lines in common with another, and so on. In this way one can tenuously connect well over thirty companies through the actual toys – including Marx (the Hong Kong branch), Lone Star, Budgie, Morestone, Benbros, and even Tootsietoy – rather than through any corporate involvement.

GERMAN DOMINATION AGAIN

So the post-war scene was frenetic, competition was fierce, and not even the fittest always survived. Outstanding among the better quality small white-metal kit producers are D.G., Western and Superscale, but there are many other very worthy but low-volume producers. All of these (unlike Lesney and Dinky Toys) are priced for the adult market, and most are too fragile to survive the nursery floor even if the average child possessed the skill necessary to assemble them.

The same remarks also apply to plastic kits, popular in the 1/32 scale but available in other scales, including the miniature and excellent Jordans in 1/87 scale. While the plastic kit market started in the US, it is now dominated – in the H0 (1/87) scale – by East and West German and Austrian manufacturers, most of whom manage to produce something like one hundred new models a year, while most of the plastic 'readymades', ostensibly of US manufacture, are actually made in Hong Kong.

Wiking, notable for having made plastic models just pre-war, built aircraft recognition models for the Luftwaffe up to 1945, subsequently perfected injection moulding techniques, and are now among the most highly respected of the German manufacturers. It is true, however, that despite the fact that plastic models are able to reproduce more detail with greater accuracy, there is still a tendency for collectors to favour white-metal models as being of greater 'substance' than plastic.

OVER-PRICED AND TOO LARGE

The cheap popular plastic kits – once epitomised by Revell, Airfix and Frog – have now tended, however, to 'go upmarket' (and become much larger), and are in danger of pricing themselves out of the market for which they were designed. New experimental materials, including polyester resins, are, however, now being tested by some manufacturers, and we may shortly see an entirely new generation of models.

It seems likely, however, that white-metal models (where capital and production costs are low for small runs – but metal-expensive) will continue to dominate the small-volume market. Plastic, on the other hand, with high capital costs in equipment, will rely on mass production. Whether the present output of up to one hundred new models a year from each 1/87 scale kit manufacturer can possibly continue, however, is a moot point. The 'Swap Meet' – an American innovation which provided a forum on which collectors could meet, swap and buy from one another, and which 'peaked' in 1980 – is losing popularity in Britain. This underlines the basic difference between the slot-racing fraternity (and the new generation of radio-controlled – R/C – model enthusiasts who have taken their place), and the toy and model collectors.

The slot racers are gregarious; the collectors more probably 'loners'. True, one is still treated to the spectacle of middle-aged German collectors earnestly but furtively conducting clandestine 'swap meets' from the boots of their cars in public car parks in Germany, and with one eye on the next bargain and the other on the Inspector of Taxes, but most of the real toy and model collectors or experts – David Pressland, Ed Force, A. Turner and David Filsell, to name a few – tend to operate in isolation rather than as part of a group activity.

Like slot racing, radio-controlled model cars (or R/C as they are better known) originated in the United States and are now well established in Britain too. Enthusiasm has not, as yet, reached the level once enjoyed by

97

the slot racers, but this is probably due to the current economic recession, and it is likely that the sport will develop its full potential later.

THE COLLECTING CATEGORIES

Collecting can, therefore, be divided into a number of categories:

Tin-plate toy collectors, who do not seek accuracy of either scale or detail, but who see in their collections either the charm of a bygone age or that of the toy itself as an art form.

Die-cast and white-metal toy and model collectors, who do demand accuracy of scale and detail (usually 1/43 scale), who prefer to be able to identify the make of vehicle which formed the prototype of the model or toy, and who require a more substantial representation (i.e. a product which 'bulks well') than those provided by plastic toys or kits.

H0 scale plastic kits purchased mainly by H0 scale (1/87) railway modellers as accessories for their layouts, or by 'collector maniacs' whose main object is to collect every model produced by the manufacturer(s) in whom they are interested. There is in this latter category something of the 'magpie' syndrome which is also present in those who are general collectors.

General toy and model collectors, of whom some (but by no means all) collect and hoard anything and everything, while at the same time acquiring little or no knowledge of the subject. Others acquire an encyclopaedic knowledge in general or specialist areas which, with the advent of the specialist press, they are sometimes prevailed upon to share eruditely with others. Often, these specialist magazines provide the only point of contact for all of the above categories.

Slot racing and R/C enthusiasts derive their pleasure from *group* activity – racing, meetings, competitions, scratch building, clubs and inter-club rivalry – although they also receive the necessary coverage in magazines which cater for the other categories.

Thematic collectors fall into a number of groups. Some concentrate only upon a single make or model of prototype full-size car – the Austin Seven or Model 'T' Ford, for example – in all its manifestations. Others will confine themselves to promotional models, i.e. those made specially for a motor manufacturer, and distributed at press launches for a new model to the press, dealers and customers. The Studebaker models made by National

Products in the US fall into this category, but sometimes special issues of popular lines by mass producers (Tootsietoy, Dinky Toys, Corgi) have been used for the same purpose.

Others might concentrate their efforts on fire engines and fire fighting equipment, but two groups deserve special mention. They are those whose main interest is *buses* and those who specialise in *military vehicles*. The first of these groups are highly organised and, with their international Model Bus Federation, are the exception which proves the rule concerning the 'lone' collector. The MBF has regional chapters in plenty and a high degree of group participation.

Military vehicle enthusiasts are different again, tending to overlap in some cases into 'war games' and into the periphery of the Military Vehicle Preservation movement, war museums, and all the subculture which this entails.

In fact, to summarise, the whole area of toy and model vehicle collecting is a series of subcultures, all with their hierarchies of experts and their following of devoted disciples. It is not until one looks below the surface that even an inkling of the vast knowledge required in each field can be properly grasped, and the rigid lines of demarcation which sometimes exist between groups can be fully appreciated.

Some collectors will not look at a model unless it is 'scratch-built', others will only be interested in something – either model or toy – which is factory made, while there is an élite who collect only models made by a *Master Modeller*. These are few and far between, and most of them produce design exercises for the actual toy and model manufacturers and the various prototypes (in the accepted sense of the word) of models and toys intended to be produced.

They will, however produce models to order, and prominent in this exclusive field are the racing cars made by Michel Conte, and the superb creations of G. H. Deason and Gerald Wingrove. Wingrove's tulipwood Hispano-Suiza, and the 1912 Russo-Baltique built for *Automobile Quarterly* magazine set new standards of excellence. But these models are for the few, costing as they do thousands rather than tens of pounds, and they are mentioned here only to complete the picture.

Sandwiched (sometimes uncomfortably) between the home assembler/scratch builder and the Master Modeller, however, is the *professional assembler/modifier*. Often (as was Jim Varney) the proprietor of a white-metal kit firm, this person will build up his own kits to be sold complete (and proportionately more expensive) or will modify an existing range of models for semi-mass sale. Thus, many Lesney basic models are modified to give greater variety/detail as demanded by the scale-model enthusiasts. In some instances, however this modification extends only to the provision of a wide range of non-original transfers (as in the case of those supplied by 'Smokey' Robinson on Lesney's Model 'T' and Talbot vans).

There are clubs in existence for all categories, and some of them are very active. Others, however, come and go and the *representative* listing of clubs shown in Appendix IV are those which were current at the time of going to press.

Obviously, with such a wide spectrum of interest in toy and model vehicles (and toys and models generally), there is an established dealer market servicing it (as opposed to the pure toyshop for children), but as dealers come and go it is probably more useful to rely upon the current issues of the various specialist magazines for details. For this reason no listing of dealers is given in this book.

Inevitably in the space available we have been able only to 'scratch the surface', since the ramifications of this fascinating hobby extend to all corners of the world. We have not mentioned the miniature cast-metal toys made in Canada by London Toys and New Market Manufacturing Co. of Ontario, nor yet the Russo-Baltique and other Russian die-cast models available from the Russian Shop at 278 High Holborn, London WC1. A whole galaxy of manufacturers exist in Czechoslovakia and other Soviet bloc countries, concentrating on die-cast (as well as tin-plate) toys and models, and there are groups of enthusiasts indigenous to those countries.

To those of you whose favourite maker or model has received but scant or no mention, our apologies. The problem throughout has been what to leave out rather than what to include, and a representative selection has been attempted. We hope that the various appendices will prove helpful if only as a quick checklist or source of reference, and that any errors and omissions will be forgiven.

Two examples of Dinky Toys 25D series petrol tanker. Both are of pre-war manufacture (and that on the left is suffering from slight metal fatigue, a Dinky failing) and are still shod with their pre-war white rubber tyres. This cannot be taken as a firm indication of date in all cases, however, since tyres can be changed. The Power version is in dark green with black chassis and blue hubbed wheels with the transfer in gold, while the Wakefield Castrol example is green and black with a red and black transfer. D, U (left); S, U (right).

Wood was not an uncommon material for even small toys such as these, which are German in origin (Erzgebirge region) and c.1920/30. During the Second World War particularly, when raw materials were in short supply, and in the frugal years immediately following, a number of British and American companies offered toy kits in wood. These included Wilson Lorries in Britain and Hudson Miniatures in the USA. M, U. (Museum of Childhood)

This cheap plastic saloon of American inspiration is, in fact, of British manufacture, and has a tin-plate base. It also relies on a friction/flywheel drive, and the damage to the rear wheel arch is typical of the inherent weakness of these early plastic toys. D, U.

This little Edwardian smoker's set looks a good deal more modern than some of its contemporaries, being more stylised in design. It incorporates a cigar cutter, vesta holder, ashtray and a headlight in which both cigars and cigarettes can be stubbed out! M, U. (Peter Richley Collection)

This attractive post-war die-cast model in 1 : 43 scale depicts the 1948 Lago Talbot coupé, and was made by the Italian firm Idea 3. As can be seen, the detail and production is good – quite as good, in fact, as that of the volume manufacturers. M, R.

A modern, scratch-built, amateur-made model of a Model 'T' Ford. With the exception of the hood, the detail is remarkably accurate, even down to the 'mother-in-law seat' and acetylene generator on the running board. This model was sold at Sotheby's Belgravia in March 1979. S, R.

Not Dinky Toys and not made in Britain. The lettering and transfers on these diecast toys give the game away, since all are made in Israel. The two Willys commercials and the Ford Prefect are by Gamda, while the Chevrolet police car and ambulance carry the Gamdakoor (Sabra) label. Both companies are associated. M, U. (Tiatsa Toy Museum)

This Spanish plastic kit (unpainted in grey) is simple, yet aesthetically pleasing, and captures the spirit of the prototype very well indeed. Depicting a Bullnosed Morris Cowley of the mid-1920s (one headlamp is missing), it is complete down to scuttle-mounted horn and Motormeter on the radiator cap. E, R. (Tiatsa Toy Museum)

Chassis detail of a Mercedes W.163 racer from Casadio. Many kit firms – particularly those catering for the slot or radio-controlled car market – offer either chassis or racing 'shells' to enable the enthusiast to 'build-in' his own running gear or bodywork as the case may be. M, R.

Military modellers are also well catered for. Mayes Models of Emsworth offer this 1920 Rolls-Royce armoured car in kit form, and similar vehicles are available from other firms. This one is based on an actual vehicle seconded to the Irish Army and named after an Irish patriot, Tom Keogh. M, U.

Perhaps no modern kit firm has done more to popularise plastic kits then Brumm. This model of Cugnot's steam wagon – the first commercial vehicle to run under its own power – is a typical example of the general quality and detailed accuracy which they offer. M, C.

One of the most well-known and popular die-cast toys of the post-war period, Mettoy Playcraft's Corgi model of Chitty Chitty Bang Bang, the star of the United Artists film of the same name. Portrayed in the film as a 'magical' car which could fly and perform other remarkable feats, it was a popular children's toy, and the Corgi model incorporated much detail (including the concealed 'wings' which would flick out at the touch of a lever). Interestingly, the bonnet was of lithographed tin plate. E, U.

Tin plate made way for many other materials in the immediate post-war period, and all three of these toys are of 'alternative' materials and North American in origin. On the left is a convertible in hard rubber or composition by Auburn (United States), the Fire Chief's car in the centre hails from Canada, and is in plastic by Viceroy, while the red and yellow sedan at the far right is from Sun Rubber Company of the USA. M to E, U. (Tiatsa Toy Museum)

Models of Yesteryear Y-15 1930 PACKARD DIETRICH **"MATCHBOX"**

LESNEY PRODUCTS & CO. LTD. LEE CONSERVANCY ROAD. LONDON. E.9
01-985 5533

An advertisement by Lesney for their 1930 Packard with coachwork by Dietrich in the Matchbox 'Models of Yesteryear' series. The Matchbox trademark was originated by the Kohnstam family, whose Moko tin-plate toys were popular before the war. Lesney acquired the Moko interests (and the Matchbox name) in 1959. M, U.

Glass containers in the shape of vehicles were pioneered in the United States during the 1930s by such firms as Victory. These three are of more modern vintage, however, having contained after-shave lotion from the Avon cosmetics firm. M, U. (Peter Richley Collection)

107

Commemorative bronzes are nowadays highly sought after, and cost a great deal of money unless a collector is very lucky. This example commemorates the exploits of Captain G. E. T. Eyston in the record-breaking M.G. at Pendine Sands. Good bronzes can be found in the Khachadourian Gallery in London or at sales organised by Sotheby's, or Christie's, or other auction houses. S, R.

Typical of the better made, popular, low-priced kits on offer during the 1960s is this Airfix Alfa Romeo in 1 : 32 scale. Based on the car once owned by the late Mike Hawthorn, the kit comprised 116 pieces and cost only 4s.3d. (pre-decimal) in toy and model shops and from Woolworth stores. M, U.

Another of Gerald Wingrove's projects. The engine of a 4½ litre 'Blower' Bentley, complete in all its detail, sits in the palm of his hand awaiting installation in the complete chassis he also built. Standards like this are rarely encountered, yet there is a surprising number of gifted amateurs turning out work just as good. Prices of a complete model would, however, be measured in thousands of pounds. M, R.

In the last ten years the low-volume white-metal kit market has boomed, particularly in Britain. This beautifully detailed Albion platform truck is by Superscale and includes transmission and radiator badge (readable!). Other models in the range include a Shelvoke & Drewry refuse collector and the Tate & Lyle McCurd lorry. M, C.

A selection of die-cast (seats and some other items are plastic) 'Models of Yesteryear' by Lesney. Although produced primarily as toys, and in large numbers, these models are very detailed and well made. Unfortunately, Lesney, from being market leaders in the 1960s, have now fallen from favour. Current models pay less attention to authenticity of colouring, tyre size and other important details, and the company have also had financial difficulties. M to S, C.

Some early pre-war Dinky Toys (note the all-metal wheels on the van and truck, and perished white rubber tyres on the other types). The Sharp's Toffee van is the 28/2 series announced in October 1934; the double decker in blue and cream series 29c of 1938; and the truck is series 22. The cars are, left to right, British Salmson (36f), Humber Vogue (24d) and Rover (36d). S to E, U.

In this selection of mainly pre-war toys, both die-cast and tin-plate types are represented. At top left is the extremely rare silver and black La Salle by Tootsietoy, the great American rivals of Dinky Toys, who entered the die-cast arena in 1932. The tin-plate 'Tricky Taxi' is by Marx, but shares pressings in common with some pre-war Schuco toys. The gangster's car and the penny toys are unmarked. E, R (La Salle); S, U (rest). (Tiatsa Toy Museum)

'Penny toys' from all periods, and in various materials. On the left, a chromed German saloon (also issued in colour and lithographed), a Russian wooden toy (modern) and a mid-1920s tin-plate charabanc made in Germany (probably part of a board or track game). On the right, a wooden toy from Taiwan, a mid-1920s tin-plate toy by Distler but issued by Essdee, and a modern Italian pottery racing car. In the centre, a mid-1950s key-ring novelty and a tin-plate Super Mini from Taiwan. M to E, U (1920s); M, U (rest).

111

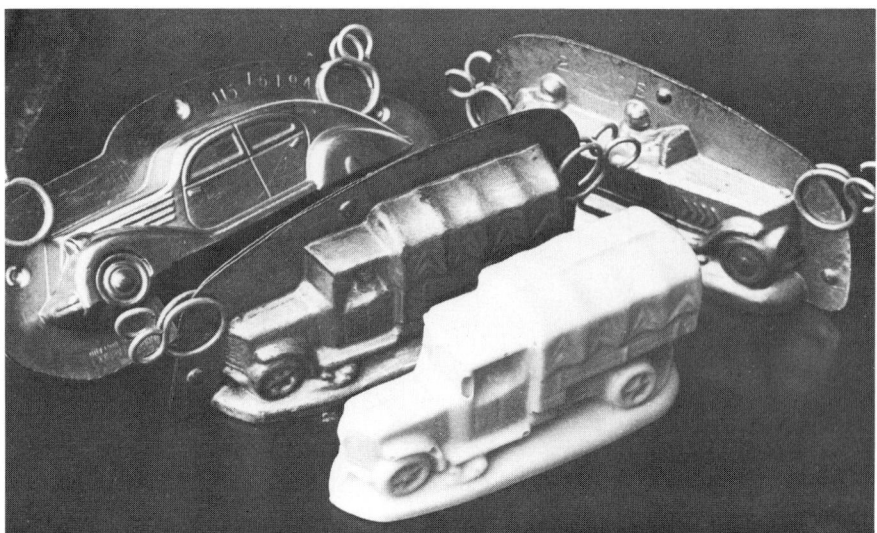

These German alloy moulds date from the 1930s but are not moulds for slush cast toys. Their purpose was to produce chocolate novelty sweets for children in the shape of a saloon, a racing car and a truck. Rarely encountered in Britain (although some jelly moulds have an automobile theme), a continental 'flea market' would be your best chance of finding some like these. M, R. (Peter Richley Collection)

Inkstands are another favourite subject for thematic collectors. This example features a very life-like chain-driven racing car, complete with begoggled driver and mechanic looking suitably dramatic, and raising clouds of dust. S, R.

The M.G. Midget epitomised the British small sports car of the 1930s, and in those days it was still fashionable for sportsmen and women to smoke. Only natural, therefore, that this ingenious little chromed M.G. should incorporate cunningly a cigarette lighter. Watch country sales for items like this – or try Sotheby's and Christie's and be prepared to pay highly. M, I. (Peter Richley Collection)

A simple chromed trophy of the type which would have been given by a regional motor club during the 1930s for an event organised for its members. Depicting a stylised saloon of the period, it is an attractive and not over-expensive item. A thematic collection of similar trophies would make an interesting display. M, R.

Dinky Toys 28 series van dating from the mid-1930s and bearing a transfer advertising Meccano, the parent company. Painted yellow, with plated radiator surround and all-metal wheels, early examples like this are not often encountered in such good condition. Prices in the market can average £150–£200 but it is still possible to find them more cheaply in jumble sales and second-hand shops. Watch large country house sales too, for the contents of that long-forgotten nursery. S, U.

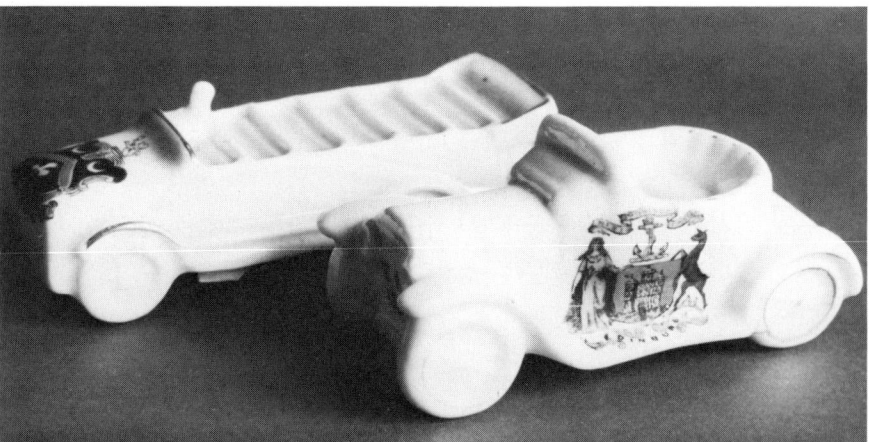

There was a time when cheap crested china could be purchased for a few pence in the local junk shop, but with the rise in interest in Goss china in particular, all crested items have now become collectors' pieces. Transport, like this charabanc and two-seater car, is a favourite theme and includes an ambulance, petrol pump, petrol can, aeroplane and Mk V tank. Not all crested china is Goss. There were many other potteries offering similar items and prices range from £4 to £35 depending on maker and condition. D, U.

This beautifully detailed model of a Leyland furniture van is typical of the industrial models made by Bassett-Lowke during the 1920s. It was commissioned by Maples, the furniture people, for advertisement purposes, and has recently been totally refurbished for Maples, Waring & Gillow by Bassett-Lowke (Railways) Ltd, the successors of the original company. M, I.

Cars made in pottery are quite often encountered, and both this Renault and its companion are of relatively recent date. They are attractive, however, and in due course, because of the less durable nature of their construction, survivors will become rare. A thematic collection of motoring ceramics would be an unusual and rewarding occupation, and much is available in Goss and other crested china. M, U. (Peter Richley Collection)

At the top end of the kit market is this very attractive looking Mercedes-Benz drophead coupé by Englan. With rubber tyres, fabric hood and upholstery, opening bonnet, wire wheels and a wealth of detail, it is a far cry from the simple Airfix and Frog models which once cost less than 5s. M, U.

A selection of toys from the immortal Dinky range, encompassing the equestrian, military, municipal, public service, commercial, racing and passenger vehicle field. It is this enormous versatility, coupled with accuracy of scale and faithful likeness to prototype, which gave the Dinky toy its universal appeal – at first to children and latterly to adult collectors. S to E, C.

In 1934 the Post Office introduced a Morris Commercial van specially bodied by Duple and intended to publicise the Air Mail service. It was used for promotional work during 1934 and 1935 and then withdrawn. Dinky Toys offered this faithful reproduction late in 1935 and it is now very rare. Painted blue, it carries the transfer in silver, and the crown and posthorn in gold. M, R.

This charming Edwardian hand mirror cleverly utilises the mirror to simulate the car's windscreen, and gives an illusion of depth. In fact, it is almost three-dimensional. Although items like this are rare, similar domestic artefacts with a motoring flavour can be found at autojumbles. A toast rack in the shape of a car and dating from the same period was found at Beaulieu in 1982 for only £4. S, R. (Peter Richley Collection)

These small spelter models were once widely available in cheap novelty shops, seaside souvenir arcades and as prizes at fairgrounds in the period up to the First World War. These models are a pin cushion and a money box, but there were a number of variations on this theme. The metal is subject to fatigue if exposed to extremes of temperature, but cheap examples can still be found in antique markets. E, U.

Back in the Edwardian era, someone conceived the bright idea of offering scale models in metal of the Rolls-Royce Silver Ghost to actual purchasers of the real car. This attractive survivor is said to be one of only about fifty made before the whole charming scheme came to an end; c.1910. M, I. (Tiatsa Toy Museum)

Interesting containers in the shape of vehicles are still being made, and this charming ½ lb storage tin is by Ian Logan Associates and made in Britain. It is lithographed to a high standard to represent an open-topped London bus of the 1920s, and exudes period charm. The other bus is in cardboard, and is issued by Cadbury's as a gift wrapping for their 'Double Decker' chocolate bars. M, U.

This Spectrum patrol car is both die cast and plastic and, unusually for a Dinky Toy, has a friction drive mechanism. Marked Dinky Toy 103, it was, in fact, made by Meccano under licence for Century 21 (Vickers Toys Ltd); c.1964. M, U (Museum of Childhood)

This superb scratch-built metal model was made by Master Modeller Gerald
Wingrove for the magazine *Automobile Quarterly* in America. It is a faithful reproduction of the Russo-Baltique which won the 1912 Monte Carlo Rally – even down
to its herring-bone pattern Prowodnik tyres. A 1: 15 scale model for which data
was supplied by Allec Ulmann of the USA and the Moscow Polytechnic Museum.
M, R.

Wills Finecast offer a selection of well-produced and finely detailed metal kits in
1 : 24 and 1 : 43 scale, and this K3 model M.G. of the 1930s is typical. Complete
down to folding windscreen and outside exhaust, it is unmistakably M.G., and it
is this concentration upon scale and an authentic likeness to the prototype which
underlines the main difference between die-cast and tin-plate toys and models.
M, U.

Despite its archaic appearance, this cigarette lighter in gun metal is of quite modern manufacture. Detail is quite good, however, and it is eminently collectable. Novelties like this are still being made, and you should not spurn them just because they are not old. In time they will be just as rare and sought after as the really early types. M, U. (Peter Richley Collection)

This decorated toffee tin by Richard & Co. is of modern manufacture but nevertheless has a period charm all of its own. Many gift shops are now offering containers of this kind at very reasonable prices, and the quality of the lithography is very high. The Royal Mail van is unusual in that it is made of cardboard and incorporates on its roof a calendar, which dates it as 1981. Given away as a Postal Service PR gimmick. M, C (left); M, U (right). (Tiatsa Toy Museum)

An advertisement for Dinky Toys' 'Gabriel' Model 'T' Ford – an example of a toy being based on a well-known character. Dinky Toys had by this time lost their market lead to Lesney, and this example incorporates a good deal of plastic in its construction – particularly in the wheels, M, U.

APPENDIX I

BIBLIOGRAPHY AND RECOMMENDED READING FOR SERIOUS COLLECTORS

AFX Road Racing Handbooks, Vols I, II and III
Antique Automotive Collectibles. Jack Martells (USA 1980)
The Art of Making Miniature Models. Daniel Puiboube
The Art of the Tin Toy. David Pressland (New Cavendish 1976; since reprinted)
Autohobby. Marco Bussi
Automobile Quarterly's Complete Book of Automobile Hobbies. Beverley Rae Kimes (AQ 1981)
Automobile Year Book of Models, No. 1 and No. 2 (Edita: Lausanne per Patrick Stephens Ltd)
Automobilia: A Guided Tour for Collectors. M. Worthington-Williams (Batsford 1979)
Auto Modely. Vladimir Prochazha (Prague 1972)
Auto World Model Cars and Trucks Catalogue (Auto World)

The Boys Book of Hobbies. Carlton Wallace (Evans 1951)
The Boys Book of Working Models. R. H. Warring (Lutterworth 1962)
British Diecasts: A Collector's Guide to Toy Cars, Vans and Trucks. G. M. K. Thompson (Haynes) (not to be confused with Frank Thompson's *Catalogue of Model Cars* (Mason 1978) which is NOT recommended)
Building and Operating Model Cars. W. A. Musciano (Funk & Wagnallis, NY 1956)
Building '00' Scale Commercial Road Vehicles. Derek Waugh and David Jane
Bulldog: The World's Most Famous Truck. John B. Montville (includes models)

Cardboard Engineering. G. H. Deason (MAP 1958/70)
Car Racing by Radio Control. G. Sipsoss (MAP 1970)
Catalogue of Toy Fire Apparatus. Vols I and II. R. Coleman and R. Russell (Phenix Tech. Inc.)
Collecting Meccano Dinky Toys
Collecting Model Farm Toys of the World. R. E. Crilley and C. E. Burkholder
The Complete Book of Building and Collecting Model Automobiles. Louis H. Hertz (Crown Publishers, NY 1970)
The Complete Book of Model Car Building. Dennis Doty (TAB Books)
The Complete Book of Model Raceways and Roadways. L. H. Hertz (Temple Press 1964)
Complete Car Modeller. Gerald Wingrove (New Cavendish 1978)
Corgi Toys: The Ones with Windows. Jas Weiland and Ed Force

Dinky Toys: Masterpieces in Miniature 1951–1958. Tony Stanford
Dinky Toys: The Favorite Collecting Hobby. Tony Stanford
Discovering Toys and Toy Museums. Pauline Flick (Shire 1971)

Electric Model Car Racing. D. J. Laidlaw-Dickson (Museum Press 1965)

F. A. O. Schwartz Toys Through the Ages 1911–1971
Frank Hornby – the Boy who Made $1,000,000 with a Toy. M. G. Gould

Games and Toys Trade Directory (particularly pre-war editions)
The Golden Age of Toys. Jac Remise and Jean Fondin (Edita: Lausanne, per Patrick Stephens Ltd)
The Great Toys of Georges Carette (catalogue reprints with commentary by Allen Levy) (New Cavendish)

The Handbook of Old American Toys. L. H. Hertz
Historic Racing Car Models: Their Stories and How to Make Them. Frank Ross Jnr
The History of British Dinky Toys (MAP 1966) (reissued Mikansue 1973)
The Hornby Companion Series (New Cavendish) including the following: *The Products of Binns Road – a General Survey* (Peter Randall); *The Meccano Super Models* (Geoff Wright); *Hornby Dublo Trains 1938–1964* (Michael Foster); *Dinky Toys and Modelled Miniatures* (Mike and Sue Richardson); *The Meccano System and Special Purpose Meccano Sets* (Jim Gamble); *The Hornby Companion – an Anthology of Meccano Ltd's Literature* (edited by Allen Levy)
How to Go Car Modelling. Gerald Scarborough

Lesney Matchbox 1–75 Series Diecasts. Maurice A. Hammond

Making Miniature Road Vehicles. J. T. Hill (Modelcraft 1947)
Making Model Trucks and other Commercials. Gerald Scarborough
Mechanical Tin Toys in Colour. Arno Weltens (Blandford 1977)
Messrs Ives of Bridgeport. L. H. Hertz
Miniature Car Construction. Cyril Posthumus (Percival Marshall 1949)
Mini Car Collection (die casts). Japan
Minic: Lines Brothers' Tinplate Vehicles. Sue Richardson (Mikansue)
Model Car Collecting. F. Brian Jewell (1964)
Model Car Directory. Foss
The Model Car Handbook. P. Plecan (1965)
The Model Car Handbook. Bob Cutter
Model Car Manual. G. H. Deason (Drysdale 1948)
Model Car Promotional and Kit Guide. Bender
Model Car Racing: Radio and Tabletop. Robert Schleicher
Model Car Rail Racing. D. J. Laidlaw-Dickson (MAP 1957)
Model Cars. Richard Knudson
Model Cars (English edition of Italian original translated by Cecil Gibson) (Orbis 1970)
Model Cars (Consumer's Guide)
Model Cars Encyclopaedia. D. J. Laidlaw-Dickson (MAP 1971)
Model Cars in Colour. Norboru Nakajima (Japan 1967)
The Model Cars of Gerald Wingrove. Gerald Wingrove (New Cavendish 1979)
Model Cars of the World. Norboru Nakajima
Model Cars of the World, Vol. 2 – *Europe.* Norboru Nakajima
Model Cars of the World, Vol. 3 – *Japan.* Norboru Nakajima

The Model Cars You Threw Away
Model Car, Truck and Motorcycle Handbook.   Robert Schleicher
Model Commercial Vehicles.   Cecil Gibson
Modellautos Aus Eigener Hand.   Wolfgang Schmarbeck
Model Race Cars.   D. A. Russell and D. B. M. Wright (Drysdale Press 1945)
Model Racing Cars.   N. Taylor (1958)
Model Road Racing Handbook.   Robert Schleicher (1967)
Motor Modelling.   Rex Hays (Arco 1961)
Motor Racing in Miniature.   G. H. Deason (Drysdale 1947)

Painting and Detailing Model Buses.   Chris Hall
Past Joys.   Ken Botto (toy vehicles 1920–50)
Plastic Model Car Kit Directory.   Samuel Richardi
Plastic Model Cars.   Cecil Gibson (MAP 1962)
The Price Guide and Identification of Automobilia.   Gardiner and Morris (Antique
   Collectors' Club 1982)
The Price Guide to Metal Toys.   Gardiner and Morris (Antique Collectors' Club
   1980; since reprinted)

Racing Cars in Miniature.   Rex Hays (Percival Marshall 1951)
Radio Control Electric Model Cars.   D. J. Laidlaw-Dickson (L.D. Editorial and
   Technical Services)
Repertoire Mondiale.   C. Veran (1958)

Scale Model Cars.   Harold Pratley (MAP 1956)
Scale Model Trucking.   Gary Nash and Mic Greenberg
Simple Electric Car Racing.   V. E. Smeed (MAP 1965)
Slot Car Racing.   Phil Drackett (Souvenir 1968)
Slot Racing.   Braverman and Neuman (1965)

Table Top Car Racing.   R. F. Dempewollf (Allen & Unwin 1963)
Technical Journal of Model Car Racing.   Mort Waters (Car Model 1967)
Tin Toys 1945–1975.   M. Buhler (Bergstrom & Boyle)
Tootsietoys: World's First Diecast Models.   James Weiland and Ed Force
The Toy Collector.   L. H. Hertz
Tribute by Trophy. Rex Hays (McGibbon & Kee 1961)

World Catalogue of Model Cars.   J. Greilsamer and B. Azema (Edita: Lausanne per
   Patrick Stephens Ltd 1967)
The World's Model Buses (Pirate 1970)
World Model Car Book.   Danhausen (1981 and 1982, Aachen, West Germany)
The World of Model Cars.   Guy R. Williams (Andre Deutsch/Geo. Rainbird)
The World of Model Cars.   Edited by Vic Smeed

Your Book of Model Car Racing.   K. E. Gee (1965)

A REPRESENTATIVE SELECTION OF JOURNALS AND MAGAZINES, BOTH PAST AND PRESENT, OF INTEREST TO TOY AND MODEL COLLECTORS

Aeromodeller (mainly during the Second World War)
After the Battle Magazine (Plaistow Press)
Argus de la Miniature (Le Pecq, France)
Auto Modeller
Auto World

Car Collector
Car Model
Car Model (New Jersey)
C.A.R.S. (Millbrae, California; definitive 'collectors only' publication)
Classic and Sportscar (Haymarket Publications; most issues have a section devoted to new models and toys)
Collector's Gazette (Publ. Weiss, Sutton-in-Ashfield, Notts)
Confectioner's Journal (USA; featured toys packed with sweets)
Craft, Model and Hobby Industry

Engine Collectors' Journal (Colorado)

Four Small Wheels (Publisher Brian Harvey; Grand Prix Models, Radlett)

H0 Auto Inf. (magazine of the Club der H0 Automodell-Freunde, Germany)

Light Steam Power (Isle of Man)
Little Cars Quarterly (BMW models only; affiliated to BMW Car Club of US)

M.A. Collection (Michel Sordet, Geneva, Switzerland)
Meccano Magazine (MAP and various publishers)
Miniature Auto (incorporated with *Model Cars* 1968)
Miniature Autoworld
Model Auto Review (R. & V. Ward, Leeds)
Model Bus Journal (published by the Model Bus Federation)
Model Car Collector (Cecil Gibson)
Model Car Journal (USA; amalgamated with Model Car Collectors' Association; mainly concerned with promotion models)
Model Car News (first specialist magazine, from publishers of *Model Engineer*; edited by W. Boddy of *Motor Sport*; DSJ also had a hand)
Model Car Newsletter (Costa Mesa, California)

Model Cars (Drysdale; incorporated in *Model Maker*)
Model Cars (reintroduced by MAP)
Model Car Science (West Los Angeles)
Model Engineer and Light Machinery Review (Percival Marshall)
Modeller's World (Mikansue)
Modelli (Italy)
Model Maker (incorporating *Model Cars* and *Model Mechanic*)
Model Maker and Model Cars (MAP)
Model Mechanic (incorporated in *Model Maker*)
Model Railway Constructor (a road vehicle section included; Ian Allan Publishers)
Model Railway News (incorporated in *Model Railways*)
Model Railways (MAP)
Model Roads and Racing
Motor Sport (most issues have a section devoted to new models and toys)

National Laundry Journal (USA – when owned by the Dowst family)

Old Cars Weekly (Krause Pubs, Iola, Wisconsin; articles on toys/models)
Old Motor (most issues have a section devoted to new models and toys)

Quatroroutine (Milan, Italy)

Radio Control Model Cars (incorporated in *Auto Modeller*)
Railway Modeller (Peco Publications, Seaton, Devon)

Scale Auto
The Scale Auto Enthusiast (Enthusiast Inc., USA)
Scale Modeller Magazine (North Hollywood, California)
Scale Models (MAP; incorporating *Model Cars* from 1973)

Thoroughbred and Classic Cars (IPC; articles on model/toy vehicles)
Toy Collector's News (Connecticut)
Toys (edited: Marco Bossi, Grugliasco, Italy – Volume 1 + 1 only)

Veteran Car (1968–70 a column entitled 'Mantelpiece Motoring')

Wheels and Tracks (Plaistow Press)

Yesterday's Motorist (Les Wilson, Manchester)

A REPRESENTATIVE SELECTION OF MUSEUMS, EXHIBITIONS, AUCTIONS AND FAIRS

Museums
The London Toy and Model Museum (Allen and Narisa Levy, and David Pressland)
The Museum of Childhood (Bethnal Green)
Musée des Arts et Metiers, Paris
National Model Museum Trust, The Aquarium, The Quay, Poole, Dorset
Pendon Model Museum, Long Whittenham, near Abingdon (John Ahearn display)
Science Museum, South Kensington, London,
The Smithsonian Institution, Washington DC
State Toy Museum, Nuremberg.
Tiatsa Model Centre and Car Museum, now incoporated in the London Toy and Model Museum

Auctions
Bearne's, Torquay
Bonham's, London
Christie's, South Kensington, London
Onslow's, Winchester
Phillip's, London
Sotheby's Belgravia, London
Sotheby's, Chester
Sotheby's, Pulborough
Sotheby Parke Bernet Inc
   New York and Los Angeles
Bernard Thorpe & Partners
   (incorporating Linden Alcock & Co.), Hereford

Auction catalogues are a valuable source of information for toy and model collectors.

Exhibitions and fairs
Brighton Toy Fair
British Toy and Hobby Fair, Earls Court, London
The London Toy and Model Museum – exhibitions are held here regularly, and have
   already included *Tin Toy Road Vehicles: The First Eighty Years* and *Fifty Years of Dinky Toys*
Model Engineer Exhibition
Nürnberg (Nuremberg) Toy Fair, Nuremberg, Germany
South Wales Model Show, Cardiff

SOME CLUBS AND ASSOCIATIONS CATERING FOR THE INTERESTS OF TOY AND MODEL VEHICLE ENTHUSIASTS

England
Auto Model Club, London
Basildon: meeting at the Town Centre, Studio B, Basildon, Essex
Bedford: telephone John Goode, Bedford 768138
British Collectors' Club
British Radio Car Association
Coventry Die Cast Model Club: meeting at the Community Centre, Brentwood Avenue, Finham, Coventry
Farnham: meeting at The Bat and Ball public house, Bounastone, Farnham
Hull and East Riding Vintage Toy Collectors' Association, c/o D. Deighton, 75 Taunton Road, Hull, North Humberside
International Plastic Modeller's Club (UK branch)
International Toys and Model Society (ITAMS), 7 Thorpe Avenue, Wakefield, Yorkshire
Lifford Model Car Club, c/o Steve Taylor, Hill Farm Cottage, Over, Cambs
London Model Club: meeting at New Savoy Tavern, Savoy Street, London WC2
London Toy Club: meeting at St Michael's Church Hall, Stockwell Park Crescent, London SW9
Maidenhead Scale Model Club
Milton Keynes: meeting at British Legion Club, High Street, Newport Pagnell, Bucks
Model Bus Federation, c/o B. Clark, 68 Parkstone Heights, Parkstone, Poole, Dorset
South Hants Model Auto Club, c/o Robin Allen, 45 Hillview Road, Hythe, or Derek Pringle, 30 Norton Close, Woolston, Southampton
UK Matchbox Club, c/o Ray Bush, 1 Tor Road, Hartley, Plymouth, Devon
Wycombe: meeting at The Plough, West Wycombe Village
Yorkshire Radio Control Model Racing Club: meetings at Committee Room, North Bridge Leisure Centre, Halifax, Yorkshire

Scotland
Airdrie: Les Stephen, 23 Cromarty Road, Airdrie, Lanarkshire
Caledonian Autominologists, 20 Langlees Street, Bainsford, Falkirk
VW Model Club (international club for Volkswagen modellers), 20 Langlees Street, Bainsford, Falkirk

Wales
Wales and West of England Association of Model Railway Clubs (organisers of the South Wales Model Show at Cardiff)

INTERNATIONAL

Australia
Sydney Model Car Club, New South Wales

Canada
Canadian Toy Collectors' Society, Box 116, Maple, Ontario

Czechoslovakia
M. Polak, Jeseniova 125, 13.00 Prague 3, Czechoslovakia

Germany
Club der HO-Automodell-Freunde

Holland
N.A.M.A.C., Eef van den Berg, Duiterlaan 166, 2903 A.C. Capelle aan de Ijssel, Holland

New Zealand
Model Car Collectors' Club, 7 Panmure Avenue, Dunedin

USA
American International Matchbox Club

A CHECKLIST OF TOY AND MODEL VEHICLES OF THE WORLD

This includes most of the major companies and/or their trade names, together with some additional information *when known*. It will perhaps serve to indicate the vast scope of the subject to those readers new to the world of small vehicles, and prove useful to seasoned veterans in all branches of the hobby.

The information is given in condensed form in the following order:

Name of company; country of origin; scale; material; date (and other remarks). Certain codes, as detailed below, have been adopted to save space. Thus:

Dux D 1 : 40 tp; 1 : 32/38 p (*see also* Markes)

indicates a German toymaker offering 1 :40 scale tin-plate toys and later 1 :32 and 1 : 38 scales plastic toys. The company was also known under the name of Markes.

CODE	COUNTRY		
A	Austria	ISR	Israel
ARG	Argentina	JAP	Japan
AUS	Australia	K	Korea
B	Belgium	NL	The Netherlands
BRA	Brazil	NZ	New Zealand
CA	Canada	P	Portugal
CH	Switzerland	PL	Poland
CHI	China	S	Sweden
COL	Columbia	SA	South Africa
CS	Czechoslovakia	SCA	Scandinavia
D	West Germany	SING	Singapore
DDR	East Germany	SU	USSR
DK	Denmark	TAI	Taiwan
Dn	Nuremberg or Fürth	TUR	Turkey
E	Spain	US	United States of America
F	France	YUG	Yugoslavia
FIN	Finland		
GB	Great Britain	MATERIALS	
GR	Greece	Code	
HK	Hong Kong	dc	die cast
HUN	Hungary	p	plastic
I	Italy	R/C	radio controlled
IND	India	tp	tin plate
IRAN	Iran	wm	white metal

A.B.   GR   1 : 60   p
A.B.C.   I   1 : 43   resin   (Carlo Brianzi)
Abingdon Classics   GB   (M.G. models)
A.B.S.   US   kit
A.B.S.   GB   1 : 76/43   metal kits   (now including Motorkits: G.S.,   Westward, Varney and Metalmodels)
Accucast   US   (Tootsietoy replicas)
Ace   US   ½ in.   wood kit   1940s–50s
Acme   HK   p
Acorn   GB   1 : 43/72   dc and kits   (cf. Atkinsons)
Richard and Carl Adam   D   tp   c.1895–c.1905   (Königsburg, E. Prussia; very similar to Lehmann)
Aero-Mobile   US   1920s   (clockwork and rear propellor!)
Aesthetic Specialities   US   metal/china/decanters
A.G.M.   GB   1 : 76   polyester   (Dinky Dublo copies; 1 : 43 also)
A.H.I.   JAP   dc
A.H.M.   US   1 : 86   p
Airfix   GB   1 : 32/12/86   kit, complete car, or slot
Air-Jet   US
A.K.   1 : 43   p
Albedo Forkel   D
Algrema   (parent company of Tekno)
A.L.P.I.A.   I   bakelite   post-war
Alps   JAP   tp   1948–
Alt Berlin   D   p kits   (repro Eko)
Aluminium Model Toys   US   1 : 24   promo
Alvisa   dc   post-war
A.M.   SU   tp   post-war 1950s
A.M.   (and **Am-Bo**)   I   tp and dc
Americana   GB   1 : 43   wm   (by John Day)
American Flyer   US   tp   (took over part of Ives 1929)
A.M.R.   1 : 43   wm
A.M.T.   US   1 : 25/20/12   promos, dc, etc.   (slot also 1951 on; now Ertl)
Anbrico   GB   1 : 86   wm kit
Anfoe   Dn   (trademark of Andreas Förtner and Joh. Haffner, Nuremberg)
Anguplas   S   1 : 86   p   (*see also* Minicars; some copied as Eko)
Anker   DDR   1 : 15/20   p
Aohearn   US   1 : 86   (and commercials)
Aoshima   1 : 12/24
Apollo   1 : 20   p
A.R.   F   dc/tp   1920s–50s
Arbur
Arcade   US   cast iron   pre-war
Aristo-Craft   US   (accessories for Hudson Miniatures)
Arm   dc
Arnaud   F   tp   c.1890–1900
Karl Arnold   D   tp and later p N gauge   1906–   (*see* Rapido)
Art Collection Auto   1 : 8   metal model   (Bugatti £1,200)
A.S.   Dn   (trademark of Adolph Schuhmann, Nuremberg)
Asahi   JAP   1 : 40 (and 1 : 16/43/50)   dc and tp   1950–   (*see* Tsusho and A.T.C.)
A.S.C.   JAP   1 : 43   dc
A.S.N.   Dn   (trademark of Adolph Schuhmann, Nuremberg)

Associated R/C
A.T.C. 1 : 20 metal
A.T.C. JAP/HK tp
A.T.C. JAP (*see* Asahi and Tsusho)
Atkinsons 1 : 24/32 slot shells (Associated and Acorn)
Atlas 1 : 24/80 slot kits
Atma BRA 1 : 20 p
Auburn US rubber/composition
Aurora 1 : 32 p kit; 1 : 60 dc; 1 : 70 'Cigarbox'
Austin-Kraft US p kits (also military ½ in. scale)
Authenticast GB wm kit
Auto-Builder US heavy steel (construction kit – clockwork – by Structo) 1917
Auto Hobbies 1 : 32 slot bodies
Auto-Kits 1 : 24 metal kits (also Wills)
Automec GB dc post-war ('Highway Models' series; some Dinky copies)
Auto-Models 1 : 24 metal kits
Auto-Pilen E 1 : 43 dc
Auto-Replicas GB 1 : 43 dc
Autostile I 1 : 43 wm (same as A.B.C.)
Auto-World p
Aviomodelli I p kit
Avon US
A.Y.K. 1 : 12 R/C

B.A.M. 1 : 43 wm
Bandai JAP/HK 1 : 16/20 kits; 1 : 86 Baby and tp 1950–
Barclay US cast iron, then dc pre- and post-war
Barnette F 1 : 32 p kits
Barrett & Sons GB dc (*see also* Taylor & Barrett)
Barringer Wallis and Manners 1920s (later Metal Box Co.; novelty biscuit tin makers; *see* B.W. & M.)
Bassett-Lowke GB tp 1899– (promo/industrial models; *see* Lowko)
B.C. JAP/HK 1 : 32 tp 1955 (later 1 : 63)
Beeju
Benbros GB dc (incl. Mighty Midgets; *see also* Qualitoys and Zebra)
Althof Bergmann US tp 1856–*c*.1900 (New York)
Best Box NL? (incl. copies of Lion and Majorette)
Betal GB
Betta 1 : 32 slot shells (same as Classic?)
Big (*see* Höfler)
Bild-a-Car US 1937–38 (Tootsietoy construction kit)
Hans Biller Dn tp then p 1937– (formerly with Bing)
Bing US (selling organisation only)
Gebrüder Bing Dn tp comm. 1863, toys from 1879 to 1933 (*see also* B.W. and G.B.N.; Bub took over some designs)
B.K.L. GB 1 : 76 (range of Auto-Replicas)
Black Country Models GB (Transport Replicas)
Blitz 1 : 43 metal
Blue Box HK 1 : 80/32 p
Bolz D tp (*see also* L.B.Z.)
Victor Bonnet F tp 1912– (took over Martin 1912; *see also* Vébé and V.B.)
Boycraft US 1920s (Steelcraft steel toys when sold by Sears Roebuck)
Boyd US 1 : 87 p

Brackenborough GB 1 : 76 wm (later joined Eames/Cotswold)
Bradshaw GB 1 : 76 dc then p (also Bradscar)
Brandli
Brandstätter Dn tp (*see also* Geobra)
Bren L dc
Brimtoy GB tp 1914–32 (later amalg. with Wells 1932)
Britain GB cast metal and p c 1900
Fred Bronner US
Brooklin CA 1 : 43 (later GB; Dinky copies orig.)
Geo. W. Brown US tp 1856–62 (*see also* Stevens and Brown)
Brumm I p
Karl Bub Dn/US 1851–1967 (*see* K.B., K.B.N., K.B./B.W.; taken over 1967
   by F. Tarr (US))
Buby ARG dc
Buccaneer GB 1 : 43 dc kits (G.P. models)
Buchner D tp
Buddy-L US/JAP/HK steel/p
Budgie GB dc (also called Micromodels; some models of Morestone)
Buffalo US tp mid-1920s
Bühler Bros Dn 1860– (Nuremberg from 1924; clockwork makers)
Bulldog HK 1 : 90 (assoc. Marx)
Burago 1 : 24 dc 1976 (ex-Marboys)
Burnett GB tp c.1910 (later taken over by Chad Valley)
W. Butcher & Sons GB 1930s construction kit (*see* Primus Engineering etc.)
B.W. Dn (trademark of Bing-Werke, Nuremberg)
B.W. & M. (*see* Barringer Wallis and Manners)
B.Z. slot

Cam JAP 1 : 43
Cambria 1 : 12 R/C
Campbell US 1 : 87 metal kit
Camtoy GB tp
Car Cast 1 : 43 wm
Cardini I tp (made in Omegna 1922–28)
Geo. Carette Dn tp 1886–1917 (*see also* G.C. et Cie, G.C.Co.N, G.C.N. and
   G.C.N.Co.; Bub took over some designs)
Carlisle & Finch
Carrera 1 : 24 p
Carroccio I 1930 (Milan)
Casadio
Casole Arts (*see* Gaiety)
C.C.H. GB 1 : 76 wm kit
C.D. F lead
C. & D. Exclusiv D H0 gauge silver
Cenbola
C.F. D tp clockwork 1920s
Chad Valley GB tp and dc, post-war p 1897–
Champion F 1 : 86/66/43 dc mostly
Champion US cast iron
Champion US 1 : 24 slot kits; 1 : 32 kits
Champ of the Road US 1 : 50/40 dc
Charbens GB dc (connected with Benbros, Crescent & others)
Chassis GB slot shells

Joseph Chein US tp 1920s (*see also* Hercules for steel toys)
Cherryca (Phenix) JAP
Chico COL dc
Cigar Box 1 : 60 dc/p 1968 (made by Aurora)
C.I.J. F tp (later 1 : 43 incl.)
Cinerius P 1 : 43 (incl. Vitesse and Rebro-Vitesse)
Circuit Series GB 1 : 43 wm (made by Motorkits)
André Citroën Jouets F steel and heavy gauge tp 1923–36 (1936 taken over by C.I.J., then 1946 J.R.D.)
C.K. JAP
C.K.O. D 1 : 32 tp (trademark of Kellermann)
Clark US tp friction *c*.1904
Classic 1 : 24 slot; 1 : 32 shells (same as Betta?)
Classic Cars (*see* G.P.)
Cle F 1 : 40/48 p (Clement Gagnet)
Clifford HK
Clover K tp
C.M. HK p
Codeg D
Cofalu F dc/p
Colibri I 1 : 43
Como US p
Conbi I 1 : 43 (sold in GB by J. Day)
Concor US/DK 1 : 87 p kits (Heljan)
Condon GB dc
Conrad D 1 : 50/43 (prev. Gescha)
Consorti p
Michel Conti I Master Modeller
Converse D? tp *c*.1900
Copycat GB (Transport Replicas)
Coral HK
Cor-Cor US tp 1920s/30s
Corcoran US steel 1920s/30s
Corgi GB dc (Mettoy-Playcraft; *see also* Husky)
Cornelius W. H. Ltd (*see* Bren)
Cosmo US cast metal 1917 (copy of 1911 Dowst limousine)
Costanzo I wood (Roma 1928–)
Cotswold GB 1 : 76 wm (bought by Pirate 1982; became Sutherland)
Cox 1 : 24/32 slot
C.R. (trademark for both Roitel and Rossignol)
C.R. F tp (Charles Roitel; assoc. Cursor later)
Cragstan US (marketing company for Japanese tp toys)
Cragsvan ISR p and dc (*see* Sabra)
Crescent GB dc (connected with Charbens, Benbros, Morestone, Budgie, Gitterman and Modern Products)
Crio 1 : 43 polythene
Cromer GB 1 : 43/86 wm kits
C.S. CS 1 : 20 p
Cursor D 1 : 43/40 p

Dalia P/E 1 : 43 dc (mainly Solido copies)
Dan D 1 : 87 (commercials)
Danbury Mint GB pewter

Danhausen (*see* D-H)
Jack Daniels Graphics US 1 : 43 metal kit
Danmini 1 : 43 wm kit
Dare Devil HK
Darnell slot shell
Darric GB 1 : 72 p kit (made by Tony Brown; also sold by Marton)
Dart GB 1 : 76 metal kit (Reliant and horsedrawns)
John Day GB 1 : 43 wm kit
Daysum JAP
Dayton US tp friction drive 1920s
D.B.G.M. 1 : 32
D.C. Dn (trademark of Doll et Cie, Nuremberg)
D.C.M.T. GB 1 : 43/35 dc/m toys (Diecast Metal Toys; parent of Lone Star;
  see Toby Toys)
G. H. Deason GB Master Modeller
John Deere US 1: 16 (tractors)
Demon 1 : 12 R/C
Dent Hardware US cast iron
Deoma GB/I 1 : 80 (mostly military; also Micromodels)
Deros resin
D.G. GB 1 : 43/86 dc kit (incl. repro Dinky; Dave Gilbert)
D-H D 1 : 43 dc metal kit
Diapet JAP 1 : 76/40/25/30 dc
Dibro GB
Dinkum Classics AUS 1 : 43
Dinky Supertoys GB (large 'de luxe' model Dinky Toys)
Dinky Toys GB dc 1933– (most issues up to 1963 1 : 48 scale, then 1 : 43;
  see Meccano)
Johann Distler Dn tp 1900–62 (also 'penny' toys; *see* J.D.N., J.D. and
  Essdee)
D.M.V. DDR
Doepke US dc
Peter Doll Dn tp 1898– (Fleischmann took over 1938; *see* D.C.)
Domo I 1949 (Milan)
Dowst US cast metal 1911–1920s (later Tootsietoy)
Doyusha JAP 1 : 32 slot kits
D.R.S. I
D.T.C. 1 : 60 metal
Dubray F (ex-Modelisme)
Dubro 1 : 32 slot shell
Dugu I 1 : 43 dc and p
Durso B
Dux D 1 : 40 tp; 1 : 32/38 p (*see also* Markes)
Dyna US 1 : 87 wm kit
Dynamic slot kit
Dynamic US R/C
Dyson GB dc (copies of Taylor & Barrett)

Eames GB 1 : 76 wm dc (some ex-Brackenborough)
Hans Eberl Dn tp 1902–29 (*see also* H.E.N., Ebo Hui-Hui)
Ebo Hui-Hui (*see* Eberl)
Eclo 1 : 32 p shells
Ecol JAP 1 : 87

Edil I 1 : 43 dc
Edison US
Efsi NL 1 : 66/60 mostly
Efzet (trademark of Gustav Fischer, Zublitz)
Egee E tp post-war
E.G.M. I 1 : 35/43 dc 1956
Eheim
Eidai JAP 1 : 20/28/43 p and dc (incl. Grip and Technika; ceased April 1980)
Einco R/C
G. & J. Einfalt Dn tp 1922– (*see also* G.E.N. and Technofix; plastic later)
Eko E 1 : 43/86 p and kit (many ex-Anguplas)
Elastolin (trademark of Hausser)
Eldon 1 : 32 p shells
Elgin US cast iron 1920s
Eligor A 1 : 43 dc
Ellegi 1 : 12 p shells
Elvuria 2
Elzett Movek HUN tp 1980s
E.M.K. F p kit
Empro GB dc
Englan GB large metal kit
E.P. Dn (trademark of Ernst Plank, Nuremberg)
E.P.L. Dn (trademark of Ernst Paul Lehmann of Brandenberg, and Nuremberg from 1951)
Epokit F 1 : 43 resin
Equipe GB (*see* L.M.)
Equipe Gallors GB (French Dinky copies by Motorkits)
Erbex 1 : 87
Erie US dc metal
Ertl US 1 : 64 (mainly tractors; took over A.M.T. 1982)
Esci slot
Esdo F
Espeire DDK 1 : 50/87 p or dc
Essdee D tp pre-war (made by Distler)
Esso GB (Morestone series)
Esteokya PL
E.T. JAP tp pre-war
Ettinger Dn tp (taken over by Rissmann in 1907)
C. H. Evans & Co. US tp 1920s/30s
Evergreen Hill US 1 : 87 wm kit
Everife SING 1 : 35 p
Evrat

F.A.B. D tp post-war
Factoria (Eko in kit form)
Fadini I polyester
Fador US balsa card and wire kit 1940s/50s (similar to Hudson Miniatures)
F.A.G.E. I 1947 (Milan)
Faivre F tp 1860–c.1918 (*see also* F.V.)
Jos. Falk D tp 1897–1935 (taken over by Plank; *see* J.F. or J.F.N.)
Faller 1 : 24/87 slot kits
Jas. Fallows US tp 19th century
Fandor Dn (trademark of Josef Kraus, Nuremberg)

Farracars F 1 : 43 1968
Faster 43
Fastwheel 1 : 87/66 (*see also* Playart)
F.D.S. I 1 : 43 metal kits
F.G.T. GB dc 1946–50 (F. G. Taylor & Sons; succeeded Taylor & Barrett)
Firefox R/C
Fischer D 1 : 87
A. Fischer D tp *c.*1925
Geo. Fischer Dn tp 1903–58
Gustav Fischer D tp (*see also* Efzet)
H. Fischer Dn tp 1908–1931/2
F.J. F 1 : 45 dc commercials; 1 : 10 tp (France Jouets)
Colin Flannery
Fleetline GB wm kit
Fleetmaster GB 1 : 76 wm kit
Jean Fleischmann Dn tp 1887– (took over some Doll 1938)
Flim HUN p
F.M.
F.M. F (trademark for Fernand Martin, Paris)
Forma I 1 : 43 dc (tractors etc)
Förtner und Haffner Dn tp (*see* Trix *and also* Anfoe)
Franco
Freidag US cast iron 1920s
Frog 1 : 24/16 p (kits and motorised)
F.S.C.
Fuchs D tp (*see also* M.F.Z.)
Fujimi JAP 1 : 30 p kit
Fulgurex CH 1 : 87 (also tp and £300+ range!)
Fun-Ho NZ 1 : 80/66 dc 1963 (used some Streamlux)
'Funnies' 1930s (Tootsietoys with comic strip characters)
F.V. I 1 : 43 metal kit
F.V. (trademark of Faivre)

Gabriel Industries US (parent company of Hubley)
Gaffe
Gaiety GB dc 1930s (crib of Septoy? plated clockwork)
Gakken JAP 1 : 16 p kit
Galamite
Galgo ARG 1 : 43 metal
Gama D 1 : 43 dc and early tp (*see* Mangold)
Gamda ISR (*see* Gamda Koor)
Gamda Koor ISR 1 : 43 (*see* Sabra and Gamda)
Gardena US slot kit
Garrick GB 1 : 76 metal kit
Gasquy B 1 : 43 dc (same as Septoy?)
Gates Willard
G.B.N. Dn (trademark for Gebrüder Bing, Nuremberg)
G.C. et Cie Dn (trademark of Geo. Carette, Nuremberg)
G.C.Co.N. Dn (trademark of Geo. Carette, Nuremberg)
G.C.N. Dn (trademark of Geo. Carette, Nuremberg)
G.C.N.Co. Dn (trademark of Geo. Carette, Nuremberg)
G.D.E. I
Gely Dn (trademark of Geo. Levy, Nuremberg)

Gem I (*see* E.G.M.)
G.E.N. Dn (trademark for Gebrüder Einfalt, Nuremberg)
Geobra Dn (trademark for Geo. Brandstätter, Nuremberg)
Gerhart-Hruska DDR 1 : 87 p
Gescha D 1 : 50/87/24/43/35 dc/tp (later Conrad; *see also* G.S.N.)
Gevo CS 1 : 30 p
G.F.N. Dn (trademark of Gebrüder Fleischmann, Nuremberg)
Ghersi I 1 : 43/80 rubber/p
Gilbert US tp clockwork (*see also* Mysto-Erector)
Gilbert JAP 1 : 18 tp
Girard US tp 1920s
Gitane F (Matchbox copies)
Gitterman GB p kits (connected with Micromodels, Budgie, etc.)
G & K D (trademark of Gundka, Brandenberg)
G.K.N. Dn (trademark of Geo. Köhler, Nuremberg)
G.L.B. I tp 1920s/30s
G.M.C. (trademark of Gebrüder Märklin & Co., Göppingen)
G.M. et Cie (trademark of Gebrüder Märklin & Co., Göppingen)
G.M. & Co. (trademark of Gebrüder Märklin & Co., Göppingen)
Goo-dee US
Goody GB slush mould
Gosen 1 : 24 p slot
Goso (trademark of Christian Gotz and Joh. Fürth)
Gotz Dn tp
Gowland & Gowland US p kit 1940s/50s (pioneer firm)
G.P. Models GB 1 : 43 wm kit
G.P. Models US p slot
Grand Tourisme GB 1 : 43 wm kit (by Mikansue)
Graphic Designers GB metal kit
Grecostyl GR 1 : 48 p
Greeno R/C
Greppert & Kelch (*see* Gundka)
Grey Iron Casting Co. US cast iron 1920s– (Model 'T' Fords; decorations not toys)
Grip JAP 1 : 28 (assoc. Eidai)
G.S. GB 1 : 86 wm kit
G.S.N. Dn (trademark of Gebrüder Schmid, Nuremberg)
G.T. Models 1 : 32/24 slot shells
Guiloy E
Guiseval P/E? 1 : 32/86/66
Gulliver F dc
Gundka-Werke D tp 1920s–44 (Greppert & Kelch; G & K; similar to Lehmann toys)
Gunn GB steam metal
Günthermann D tp 1877–1964 (*see* S.G.; Siemens took over in 1965)
Gunze JAP 1 : 43 wm kit
Mery Gutmann F tp 1950s (Paris; *see also* MEMO)
G.Y.L. B 1 : 43 metal (cast by A.M.R.)

Habi D tp
Ha-Bi
Hafner US tp 1900–1930s (took over part of Ives 1929; *see* New York Flyer)
Haji JAP tp 1951– (Mansei Toy Co.)

Hales US p kits
Hales GB p kits
Hammer D 1 : 87, etc
Harbutts *c*.1914 (*see* R.L.; plasticine company who sold R.L. to Jet)
Hardray AUS dc
Harris US cast-iron clockwork pre-1914
Hartkopf D tp *c*.1930s (took over Stock)
Hasegawa 1 : 24 p
Hausser D tp comm. 1904 (plastic from 1955; *see also* Elastolin)
Hawk/Testor 1 : 32 slot kit
Heljan (known as Concor in US)
Heller F 1 : 24/20 p kits and slot
Heller und Schiller D tp –1945 (*see also* Husch)
H.E.N. Dn (trademark of Hans Eberl, Nuremberg)
Hercules US (steel models of Chein)
Heritage Collection US brass-plated 'auto banks'
Herpa D 1 : 86 p
Herr DDR 1 : 87/20 p
Mattheus Hess Dn tp flywheel mechanism 1826–1934 (*see also* Hessmobil, M.H.N., J.H.L.)
Hessmobil Dn (*see* Hess)
Heyde D? tp
HiFi I aluminium
High Speed 1 : 20 p
Highway GB 1 : 76 wm/p kit
Highway Models GB dc (*see* Automec)
Highway Pioneers (*see* Gowland & Gowland)
J. Hill GB cast lead, 2-d; and dc, 3-d
H.K. Dn (trademark of Hans Krauss, Nuremberg)
H Models GB 1 : 43 wm
Hobbycraft GB (alias S.M.E.C.)
Hobby Tecnica I 1 : 43 wm
Hodges GB wm (Dinky style; cf. Toys of Yesteryear)
Höfler Dn tp 1938–54 (then 'Big'; *see also* J.H.)
Hornby GB (*see* Meccano, Dinky Toys and Modelled Miniatures)
Hove AUS p and dc
H.P. (trademark of Hermanos Paya)
H.P.A.I. (trademark of Hermanos Paya)
Hruska DDR
H.T. HK p
Hubley US 1 : 22/18 metal kits (orig. cast iron and dc)
Hudson Miniatures US balsa, card and wire kits, $\frac{3}{8}$ in. and $\frac{3}{4}$ in.; then p kit 1940s/50s
Hudson Scott & Sons GB 1920s (novelty biscuit tins; Carlisle)
Huki Dn tp (*see also* Hubert Kienberg, Nuremberg)
Hull and Stafford US tp 19th century
Hurlimann R/C
Husch D (trademark of Heller und Schiller, Obersleutensdorf)
Husky GB dc (small Corgi range sold in Woolworth's)
H.V. D tp
H.W.N. Dn (trademark of Heinrich Wimmer, Nuremberg)
H.Y. JAP (*see* H. Yamada)

I.B. & Co. US (trademark of Ives, Blakeslee & Co., Bridgeport)
I.B. & W.Co. US (trademark of Ives, Blakeslee, Williams & Co., Bridgeport)
Ichiko JAP tp post-war
I.C.I.S. I 1 : 43 dc 1960 (?I.C.S.)
I & D R/C
Idea 3 I 1 : 43 metal
Ideal JAP 1 : 24 p
Ideal Dn (trademark of J. G. Schrodel, Nuremberg)
Idem F 1 : 43 wm kit
Igla CS 1 : 20/65 p and tp
Igra CS 1 : 43/35 p
Imai JAP 1 : 16/8 kits
I.M.C. US 1 : 25 kits
I.M.C. US (trademark of Ives Mfg Co., Bridgeport)
Impy dc (*see* Lone Star and Benbros)
Inco I (Turin 1948)
Industria Nazionale Giocattoli Automatici Padova I (*see* I.N.G.A.P.)
Industro-Motive US p kit
I.N.G.A.P. I tp pre-war, then 1 : 43/30/32/75/35 p 1919–72 (taken over by Eurotoys; Padua; *see also* Industria Nazionale, etc.)
I.N.G.A.T. I 1947 (Turin)
Inter-cars E 1 : 43 dc (at first based on Sablon; same as Nacoral)
Iron Art US
J. A. Issmayer Dn tp 1861–1933/4 (*see* J.A.J.)
Italerei I 1 : 35
I.T.C. 1 : 24 p 1951
Ites CS tp 1980s
Ives CS 1 : 23
Ives US tp 1868–1929 (taken over by American Flyer, Hafner and Lionel; *see* I.B. & Co., I.B.W. & Co., I.M.C. and I.W. & Co.)
I.W. & Co. US (trademark of Ives and Williams)
Izola YUG 1 : 87

Jab-toys F 1 : 43 wm
Jacques B
J.A.J. Dn (trademark of Johann A. Issmayer, Nuremberg)
Jato P tp
J.D. Dn tp (*see* Johann Distler)
J.D.B. dc
J de P F (J.E.P., Jouets de Paris)
J.D.N. Dn (trademark of Johann Distler, Nuremberg)
J.E.F.E. E
J.E.M.
J.E.P. F tp and dc 1958 1928–65 (orig. S.I.F.; Jouets de Paris; Jouets en Paris)
Jet GB (*see* Harbutts and R.L.)
J.F. F p
J.F. Dn (trademark of Jos. Falk, Nuremberg)
J.F.N. Dn (trademark of Jos. Falk, Nuremberg)
J.H. Dn (trademark of J. Höfler, Fürth)
J.H.L. Dn (trademark of Johann Leonhard Hess, Nuremberg)
Jibby CH 1 : 43 tp

Jimson HK p
J.K.Co. Dn (trademark of Joseph Kraus, Nuremberg)
J.K.Co.N. Dn (trademark of Joseph Kraus, Nuremberg)
J.M.L. F tp 1930s
J.N.F. Dn 1 : 43 tp (Joseph Neuhierl, Fürth; *see* Jos. Neuhierl)
J.N.T. slot shells
Joal E dc
Johillco GB dc (connected with Taylor & Barrett and D.C.M.T.; some Toot-
    sietoy copies)
Jolly Roger GB dc (Wales)
Jolly Roger GB
Joltan US 1 : 25 p kit
Jomac R/C
Dave Jones GB 1 : 43 metal kit
Jordan US 1 : 87 p kit
Jouef F tp 1919– (p post-war; Paris)
Jouet Mont-Blanc F tp post-war
Joustra F tp 1 : 16 1935– (owned by G. Marx, ex-Bing director; i.e. Jouet
    Strasbourg)
Joyboy GR H0
Joyo E (trademark for Hermanos Paya)
J.P. F p
J.R.D. F 1 : 43 dc 1958–62
J.S. Dn (trademark of Jean Schönner, Nuremberg)
Jue BRA dc (later Minimac then Supermini)

Kado JAP 1 : 43 wm
K & B 1 : 32/43 slot kits, then 1 : 86 wm
K & B.B. D (trademark of Kindler and Briel, Böblingen)
K & R
Kaneko JAP tp pre-war
Kansas Toy & Novelty US slush cast metal 1920s/30s
Kanto Toys JAP tp early 1960s
Karl DDR 1 : 50 p
Kay GB clockwork post-war
K.B. Dn (trademark of Karl Bub, Nuremberg)
K.B./B.W. Dn (trademark of Karl Bub and Bing-Werke, Nuremberg, 1933)
K.B.N. Dn (trademark of Karl Bub, Nuremberg)
K.C.O. Dn (trademark of Geo. Kellermann & Co., Nuremberg)
K.D.N. CS 1 : 20 tp 1980s
Keim Dn tp 1937–60 (took over J. Kraus & Co. and W. Krauss 1937/8)
Geo. Kellermann Dn tp 1910– (trademark C.K.O. or K.C.O.)
Kelmet US steel
Kembo GB dc
Kemlow GB
Kenda JAP 1 : 43/20 brass
Kenton US cast iron 1920s (some models similar to Dent)
Kenwater GB 1 : 76 wm kit
Kerl Line
Keyser
Keystone US steel 1920s
Kibri D 1 : 87 p kit or complete (*see also* Kindler and Briel)
Kico Dn (trademark of Hubert Kienberger, Nuremberg)

Hubert Kienberger Dn tp 1910– (also 'penny' toys; also Huki and Kico)
Kilgore US cast iron (some models similar to Tootsietoy)
Kindler and Briel D tp 1865– (p post-war as Kibri; *see also* K & B.B.)
King I 1 : 43
Kingsbury US tp/wood/cast iron 1919–45 (patent sealed clockwork motor; prev. Wilkins)
Kirby 1 : 24/32 slot shells
Kirk US/DK (seceded from Tekno 1971)
K.K. (*see* Sakura)
Kleeware p kit
Kleinbahn D
K.M.C. HK p (-Crown)
K.M.O.
Knapp
Knight p (-Petit)
K.O. JAP tp novelty mid-1960s
Kogure 1 : 12 kits
Kohler Dn tp 1932– (*see also* G.K.N.)
Moses Kohnstam Dn 1875– (wholesaler, but toys sold under Moko name)
Richard Kohnstam GB (grandson of Moses; *see* Riko)
Kokyu JAP tp pre-war
Kolner Automodell D
Komi US 1 : 25 battery powered kits
Kosuge JAP tp pre-war
Josef Kraus Dn tp 1910–37/8 (taken over by Keim; *see also* Fandor, J.K.Co. and J.K.Co.N.)
Hans Krauss Dn tp (*see also* H.K.)
Wilhelm Krauss Dn tp 1895–1938 (taken over by Keim; *see also* W.K.)
Kremli 1 : 40 p
K.R.Z. (trademark of Karl Rohrseitz, Zirudorf)
K's GB metal kit (Keyser)
K Toys JAP tp 1 : 43
S. Kumar & Co. IND (Dinky licence producers)
Kurt-Haufe DDR 1 : 87 p
Kyosho 1 : 12 R/C

L.A.C. I tp 1902–
La Ganke H0 slot
L & S JAP 1 : 16 p
Lancer US 1 : 24/32 slot bodies
Lange DK (became Tekno, then Kirk)
Langley GB 1 : 76 and N scale wm kit
Laurie HK 1 : 76 and larger p
L-Bros GB (*see* Lines Bros)
L.B.Z. (trademark of Lorenz Bolz, Zundorf)
L.C. HK p
L.D.C.W. GB (London Die Cast Works)
L.D.M. GB wm kit (record cars; Lawrence Designs & Models)
Lectricars R/C
Leebour US 1 : 87 p and metal kit
Lego SCA/I 1 : 80 p (1 : 43 1951–54)
Ernst Paul Lehmann Dn tp 1881– (*see also* E.P.L.; also 1 : 43 scale Gnom; at Nuremberg from 1951; post war also p)

Lemeco S dc 1945– (orig. Dinky copies)
Leningrad Council of National Economy USSR tp
Lenyko S dc 1958–63 (-Geno)
Lenz R/C
Lesney GB dc 1953– (connected Kohnstam re Matchbox series)
Lesney-Moko GB (trademark following absorption of Kohnstam interests in 1959)
Georg Levy Dn tp 1916–34, then Nuremberg Tin Toys Factory until 1971 (*see also* Gely; ex-partner of Kienberger)
Ley D brass (made by same company who made full-size cars)
Lightning R/C
L.I.G.I. I 1949–
Lilliput GB dc
Lilliput GB 1 : 86 card kits
L'il Old Timers US (*see* Hudson Miniatures)
Lima I 1 : 45 tp, 1 : 20/28/30 p 1946– (Vicenza)
Lincoln Hi-Ways NZ
Lincoln International HK dc
Linda HK p
Lindberg US 1 : 25/8/12/32 slot kits and plain kits (chassis only)
Linemar JAP tp novelty 1950s–60s
Lineol D tp 1934–45 (Brandenberg; mainly military)
Lines Bros GB/NZ/CA/AUS/SA steel, wood, tp, p, dc 1919–1980s (*see also* L-Bros, Tri-ang, Minic, Dinky Toys, Hornby and Meccano from 1964)
Lineside (*see* Modelcraft)
Lion NL dc (Lion-Car)
Lionel US tp 1906– (took over part of Ives 1929; now Model Products Corp.)
L.M. Replicas GB 1 : 43 wm
London CA dc
Londontoy CA dc
Lone Star GB/HK 1 : 50/35 dc, also Flyers 1 : 66, Impy 1 : 60, also p (*see also* D.C.M.T.)
Lowko (trade name for Bassett-Lowke)
L.R. Resitrex F rubber 1930s
L.S. JAP 1 : 24 slot kit
Lucky Toys HK 1 : 32 p
Luso P 1 : 43 kits
Luxor NL
Lys P 1 : 43 p

Mabri B wm kit (*not* GB; *Marc Bri*an)
Mado I
Magicars GB (made by Tri-ang)
Magnuson US 1 : 87 wm and p kit
Mai US
Mainstream (*see also* Paya)
Majorette F 1 : 86
Malvern Models GB 1 : 76 (range of John Day)
Mamod GB steel/steam
M and L US cast 1930s/40s
M & M US 1 : 87 p kit
M & S GB 1 : 43 wm kit
Mangold Dn tp 1882– (*see also* Gama and Moko; took over Trix 1971)

Manoil US dc 1934–*c*.1950s
Manon F 1 : 43 wm (Le Mans 1975–)
Marboys I 1 : 24 dc
Marc 1 : 21 p friction
Marc Europa 1 : 43 wm
Marc Europa GB wm kit (Brian Jewell)
Marchesim I 1908
Marco France F tp/p post-war
Mardave 1 : 32 slot kits
Markes D tp 1904– (p post-war; *see also* Dux)
Gebrüder Märklin D tp and kits, dc 1859– (p post-war; *see* G.M.C., G.M. et Cie and G.M. & Co.)
Marlines (trademark of Louis Marx)
Marmande
Marque wm
Marque Products
Fernand Martin F tp 1878–1912 (taken over by Bonnet et Cie; *see* F.M.)
Marushin JAP 1 : 43 (-Ministar)
Marx HK/US tp and p (HK connected with Lone Star; took over Strauss Man & Co., *c*.1920; *see also* Marlines)
Marx GB tp and p (factory at Dudley; now part of Dunbee-Combex)
Master Caster US dc, promos, etc. 1948–55
Masudaya JAP 1 : 87 p snapkit
Matai NZ 1 : 43 dc (produced Micro Models 1974)
Matchbox (*see* Lesney)
Mattel
Mattel JAP (Mebetoys)
Maxi-Jet (commercials)
Maxitoys NL tp
Maxwell IND (tractors/commercials, etc.)
May Cheong HK
Mayes GB 1 :43 wm 1980– (Milestone series; military; also L.R. cars)
M.B.L. I 1948
M.C.M. F metal kit
M.D.C. US slot
M.E. CHI tp
Mebetoys I 1 : 32/43 dc
Meccano GB tp construction kits (*see also* M.L.D.L. and Dinky Toys)
Meier Dn tp 1879–1920s (mainly penny toys)
MEMO F (*see also* Mery Gutmann, Paris)
Mercury I 1 : 32/43/48 dc 1927– (also made Speedy)
Meri
Merit GB 1 : 24 p kit
Merlin GB dc
Merlin US dc
Merriam Mfg. US tp 19th century
Merry Toys AUS dc 1940s
Metal Box Co. GB tp *c*.1914–*c*.1930s (and novelty biscuit, etc., tins)
Metal Cast Prods Co. US 1930s/40s (supplied slush moulds to smaller manufacturers)
Metalgraf I 1920
Metalgraph
Metalmodels GB 1 : 43 wm kit

Metalograph I tp 1930s
Meteor NL tp
Metosul P 1 : 43 dc
Mettoy GB tp 1934– (became Corgi dc; director ex-Tipp)
M.F.Z. (trademark of Martin Fuchs, Zirndorf)
M.H.N. Dn (trademark – early – of Mattheus Hess, Nuremberg)
Microboys I
Micro Models/Microboys I 1 : 105/125 dc (also known as Deoma)
Micromodels GB 1 : 76 card (*see* Modelcraft)
Micro Models AUS/NZ (made by Goodwood (Aus) Productions Pty, J. A. Brent & Co., Lincoln Industries 1 : 43 dc 1951–61, then NZ)
Microweight slot bodies
Midget Cars
Midget Models GB 1 : 76 wm kit (taken over by W & T)
Midge-Toy US
Midnight
Midori JAP 1 : 24 slot kit
Mighty Midget GB dc metal post-war
Mikansue GB 1 : 43 wm kit
Mi-kit GB 1 : 76 wm kit (became Motorway)
Milikits GB 1 : 66
Minerva GB tp 1920s
Minialuxe F 1 : 43 p and metal
Miniature Toys Inc. US 1 : 43 wm
Miniature Trucks Co. US ¼ in. wooden kits 1940s/50s
Mini-auto CS 1 : 43 p and metal 1960s
Mini Auto 1 : 43 metal kit
Minic GB 1 : 35/43 tp and p pre- and post-war (also Tri-ang)
Minicar
Minicars IRAN 1 : 60 p (copies of Siku)
Mini-Dinky HK 1 : 72
Mini-Lindy US (*see* Lindberg)
Minimodels GB tp clockwork 1954–56 (*see also* Starbex)
Miniracing
Minitanks A 1 : 86 p (also Roskopf)
Mini-Toys (*see* Samtoys)
Minix GB p (Tri-ang)
Mintex 1 : 43 p
Mira E
Mitsubishi I dc promos
M.K. DDR 1 : 87 p
M.K. (*see* Müller and Kadeder)
M.L.D.L. GB (trademark of Meccano Ltd, Liverpool)
M.M.N. Dn (trademark of Max Moschkowitz, Nuremberg)
M.N.N. Dn (trademark of Michael Nusslein, Nuremberg)
Mobius D dc
Mod-Ac US wood kits 1950s
Modelcraft GB card kits (plans plagiarised by later dc metal mfrs; *see* Micromodels)
Model Design Co. GB 1 : 72 p
Modelisme F (Paris)
Modelled Miniatures GB (cf. Dinky Toys, 1933 name)
Modelos P

Modelpet JAP dc
Modelpower US 1 : 87 p
Model Prods Corpn US p kits
Models 65 GB
Models of Yesteryear GB dc (*see* Lesney)
Modern Boy GB tp 2-D toys given away with this 1920s comic
Modern Toys JAP tp pre-war
Modlwood US 1913 (name for Schoenhut wooden kit)
Modsport 1 : 43 wm kit
Moko GB/D tp, probably made by Mangold (*Mo*ses *Ko*hnstam) (later Lesney-Moko)
Moline Pressed Steel US (*see* Buddy-L)
Monbandon
Monmouth GB 1 : 76 wm kit
Monogram US 1 : 24/32 slot kits; 1 : 8 p kit
Mont Blanc
Monteleone 1 : 16 p
Mopok GB 1 : 86 wm kit
Morestone GB dc (Morris & Stone; also Esso; connected with D.C.M.T., etc.)
Morgan Milton Ind. (another Dinky copy)
Moschkowitz Dn tp 1919–71 (England from 1929; *see* M.M.N.)
Mosquito (made by Solido 1952–55)
Motorific
Motorkits GB 1 : 43/76 wm (B. Garfield-Jones and Motormodels)
Motorway GB 1 : 76 (ex-Mi-kit)
Mountain States 1 : 87 p kit
M.P.C. US 1 : 24 p kit/slot
M.P.C. snapkits
M.P.W. DDR 1 : 30
M.R.F.
M.R.R.C. 1 : 32 slot kit
M.S. GB 1 : 86 wm kit
M.S. Dn (trademark of Michael Seidel, Nuremberg)
M.T. JAP tp 1924– (K. K. Masutoku Toy Factory)
M.T. JAP tp post-war (Masuya Toys)
M.T.S US 1 : 87 bus kits and wm (Model Traction Supply)
Müller and Kadedér Dn tp *c*.1900–*c*.1912 (*see* M.K.)
Multiple Toymaker US 1 : 65, etc. p
Muovo 1 : 50 p
D. Murray Wilson wooden lorry kits (*see* Wilson)
Murray Ohio Mfg US tp 1920s–30s
Mysto-Erector US construction kit (later Gilbert)

Nacoral E 1 : 43/24, etc. metal
Nagano R/C
Nakajima/Seisakiyo JAP 1 : 34/38
National US 1 : 86/43 wm kit (also promos for Studebaker)
Nat. Products 1934–50 (mostly promos; later Bantbrico)
N.A.V.A. I 1946–47 (Vimercale)
Ne-kur TUR? tp post-war
Nemo F tp
Jos. Neuhierl Dn tp 1920–56 (p post-war; also J.N.F. and Carrera racetrack)
New Market CA dc metal

New York Flyer US (trademark of Hafner Mfg Co., Chicago)
N.F.I.C. HK
N.I.C. HK
Nicads R/C
Nichimo JAP 1 : 24/32 slot kits
Nicky IND (Dinky follow-on)
Niedermeier Dn tp 1934–60s (took over Saalheimer & Strauss 1934)
Nigam I 1 : 42/43 dc 1946– (Milan)
Nitto p kit
Noch 1 : 60
Nomura JAP tp
Norev F 1 : 43/86 p and metal
North & Judd US cast iron
Nostalgic Miniatures US 1 : 50 metal kit
Novoexport USSR
Nuremberg Tin Toys Factory Dn 1934–71 (prev. Levy; Nürnberger Blechspielwarenfabrik
Nusslein Dn tp (*see also* M.N.N.)
Nyrkinen FIN 1 : 20/24 polythene
N.Z.G. D dc

Oh! Boy US 1920s (controlled by Geo. Borgfeldt & Co.)
O.K. HK p
O.K.C. F 1 : 43 wm
Old Cars I 1 : 43 dc
Omas I tp 1930s
Omicron I 1947
O.M.Y. GB rubber
Oriental JAP 1 : 86 dc
Orobr (*see* Oro-Werke Neil, Blechschmidt and Müller)
Oro-Werke D tp –1922 (*see also* Orobr; Brandenberg)
Osul P p 1964 (became Metosul)
Otaki JAP 1 : 20/24 slot kits
Ottenheimer CH 1 : 43 wm kit (also known as P Models – Peter Ottenheimer)

Pactra 1 : 24 shells
Palitoys GB p
Palmer 1 : 32/24 track kits
Paya E dc, p and tp 1906– (some Lehmann copies; *see also* H.P., H.P.A.I., R.A.I. and Joyo)
P.B. R/C
Pean F tp (*see also* P.F.)
Peelers US 1 : 43 dc (made in HK by Playart)
Peetzy (now with Roco)
Penguin GB
Penguin JAP
Pennine Chain Models GB (Transport Replicas)
Pennytoy I 1 : 66 metal
Peraboni I (*see also* S.V.P. – Peraboni)
Permot CS/DDR
Petrel HK 1 : 25 p
P.F. F (trademark of Pean Freres, Paris)

Phantom Cars R/C
Piccolo D 1 : 90 (by Schuco)
Pilen I 1 : 43 (*see also* Auto-Pilen)
Pim-Pam F tp
J. Piper Ltd 1 : 100 wm
Pirate GB 1 : 76 wm kit
Ernst Plank Dn tp 1866–1930s (taken over by Schaller Bros; *see* E.P.)
Plasbo FIN 1 : 36 p
Playart HK p
Playboy B 1 : 43 wm
Playtoy US (Tootsietoys sold through F. W. Woolworth)
Plumbies 1 : 43 wm
P.M. I (Presso-Meccanica)
P.M.C. US promos (Product Miniatures Corpn; also Tru-Miniature)
Pocher I 1 : 8 chassis kits; 1 : 13/80/16 p
Pogus S dc
Pola p kit
Policar
Polichinelle F tp
Polistil I 1 : 32/24/25/15 various metal 1974 (ex-Politoys)
Politoys I 1 : 43/25 p and dc 1960
Polmot USSR 1 : 32 card
Power-Track slot (Matchbox)
P.R.
Praline D 1 : 87 p (assoc. Walldorf)
Prameta D 1 : 32 dc
Precisia F p kit
Precision Miniatures US 1 : 43 metal
Prefo DDR
Preiser
Premier US p
Prep 1 : 87
Pressman US dc 1930s (some disputes with Tootsietoy)
Primus Engineering Motor Chassis Outfit (*see* W. Butcher & Sons)
Probar I p kit
Progetto-K
Project 1 1 : 43 wm
Pyccoba USSR dc post-war
Pyro US 1 : 32 ¾ in. scale p kit

Qualitoys GB (made by Benbros; *see also* Zebra)
Quality US 1 : 87 wm kit
Quiralu F 1 : 43 dc

Rabbit JAP tp 1950– (moto-Asakusa)
Rabro SA (Chad Valley)
Radar *P* (*Wiking copy*)
Radiguet F tp 1872–89 (later Radiguet et Massiot 1889)
Radiguet et Massiot F tp 1889–1905 (*see* Radiguet)
R.A.I. E (trademark of Paya, Spain)
Rail-Route
Railside GB (*see* John Day)
Ralstoy US dc

Rami F 1 : 43 dc
Rampini I wm/polyester (also known as Modelli R; also make Excalibur)
Ranlite GB metal/bakelite/clockwork 1931
Rapid US (*see* Scale Sundowners Ltd)
Rapido Dn (trademark of Karl Arnold, Nuremberg)
Ra-Ro I 1 : 43
Ravo JAP dc
Real Typer CA 1 : 50 (Burslem Industries, Toronto)
Record
Redondo E 1 : 24
Re-EL 1 : 10 p
Reen JAP wm kit
Reka
Reliable CA
Renewal Prods US p kits (military)
Renwall US 1 : 48/12 p
Republic US tp friction drive 1920s
Retro-MG GB wm (based on Taylor & Barrett)
Revell US 1 : 32/43 p kit; 1 : 24 slot kit
Rico E tp and p 1920– (now tp again; *see* R.S.A.)
Rieman Seabrey US steel trucks 1920s
Riggen slot
Riko GB 1 : 86 card kits; 1 : 32/24 slot kits (*Ri*chard *Ko*hnstam Ltd)
Ringo US p
Rio I 1 : 43 dc (veteran and vintage)
Rissmann Dn tp (took over Martin Ettinger 1907; *see also* W.R.)
Rivarossi I 1 : 43/75 p
River GB
Rivival I 1 : 20 dc and p
R.L. AUS 1 : 90 p veteran kits (also marketed by Harbutts Plasticine and Jet
    Petroleum)
R.N. tp 1930s
Roadace 1½ mm and 3 mm to the foot dc
Roadmaster (Lone Star series)
Roadway GB wood and card
Robeiro P tp
Robin Hood GB
Robin Hood JAP (Matchbox copies, etc.)
Robustelli
Rockford US
Roco A tp; p (*see also* Peetzy)
Rohrseitz D tp (*see also* K.R.Z.)
Roitel F tp 1880–1920 (*see also* C.R.)
Roman E tp/p
Rosedale GB
Rossignol F tp 1868–1962 (*see also* C.R.)
Les Routiers F
Roxy 1 : 20/32 p
R.S. S 1 : 43 dc 1936/7 (Reise)
R.S.A. E (trademark of Rico, Spain)
Rubicon JAP wm
Ruch PL 1 : 72 p
Russkit US 1 : 24 slot

R.W. D 1 : 43 dc

Saalheimer and Strauss Dn tp 1930s
Sablon B
Sabra ISR 1 : 43 dc
Safar I dc clockwork 1946–48 (Milan)
Safir F 1 : 43 p and metal
Sakura JAP 1 : 43 dc
Samochodzik PL 1 : 43 tp
Sampson US 1920s (sold only by Butler Bros, NY)
Samtoys I 1 : 43/45/75 p 1955–57 (also Mini-Toys)
Sankyo 1 : 24/25
Sanwa Tokyo Palma JAP 1 : 32 p *c.*1953
Savoye US slush moulded metal 1930s
S.B. 1 : 43 wm
Scalecraft GB 1 : 24/30 mastic
Scaledown GB metal kit (also Model Tractor Co.)
Scale Sundowners Ltd US 1 : 86 wm (also known as Rapid)
Scalex (*see* Minimodels; last two issues known as Starbex)
Scalextric GB ¾ in. scale slot (Lines Bros)
Scamold GB dc and kit
Gebrüder Schmid Dn tp (*see also* Gescha and G.S.N.)
Schocking
Schoenhut US all wood painted kits 1913 (first ever?; *see* Modlwood)
Jean Schönner Dn tp 1875–1907 (taken over by Falk; *see also* J.S.)
Schreyer & Co. (*see* Schuco)
Schrodel Dn tp (*see also* Ideal)
Schuco Dn 1 : 90/16, etc. p/dc 1912– (orig. tp; *see* Schreyer & Co.)
Adolf Schuhmann D tp 1925–*c.*1938 (*see* A.S. and A.S.N.)
Schumacher 1 : 21 R/C
Schwartz US cast 1911–70s (Tootsietoy cars included in Traffic Police set)
Scientific Models US
Scorpio GB polyester (Wizard; Dinky replicas)
Sebo S cast iron
Seidel Dn tp 1881– (from 1950s p; *see also* M.S.)
Septoy dc
Sery CS bakelite
Sevenuit
S.G. Dn (trademark of S. Günthermann, Nuremberg)
S.H. JAP tp 1959– (Horikawa Toys)
Shackleton GB dc (Foden trucks, etc.)
Shimer US cast iron
Shinsei JAP (incl. Mini-Power)
S.I.F. F tp 1899–1928 (Sociètè Industrielle de Ferblanterie; later *Jouets de Paris*)
Siku D 1 : 43/50/66 dc; 1 : 60 p up to 1963
Silvertone Special HK p
Silvine JAP p
Singapore Toy 1 : 20 p
Sizzlers (*see* Mattel)
Denzil Skinner GB 1 : 16/96 (mainly military in lead)
Skybirds GB lead alloy 1932–39
D. H. Slack 1 : 32 slot shells

S.L.J.
Smallster   US   (*see* Fador)
S.M.E.C.   GB   1 : 32   wood kits
Smer   CS   1 : 50/42   p
A. Smith   GB   1 : 43   promos
S.M.P   US   p
Solido   F   1 : 43   dc   (Majorette since May 1982)
Somerville   GB   1 : 43   wm
Souchis
Souvenir   HK   1 : 43   p
S.P.   F   tp   1930s
Speedy   1
Speedy   1 : 66
Spielwaren Danhausen   (*see* Danhausen)
Spot-on   GB/NZ   1 : 42   dc from 1959   (sold to Lines NZ 1968)
Stabo-car   1 : 32   p
G. L. Standt   D   tp   *c.*1840–1948   (taken over by Fleischmann)
Paddy Stanley   GB   1 : 43   dc kit
Starbex   GB   (*see* Minimodels)
Star Car   JAP   tp
S.T.D.   R/C
Steelcraft   US.   1920s   (steel by Murray Ohio Mfg; *see* Boycraft)
Stevens and Brown   US   tp/cast iron   1869–89   (previously Brown)
Stevens Bros   US   tp/cast iron   1889–1950
Stewart   US   1 : 86   wm kit
S.T.L.   F   wm and polyester   1975–   (Lyon)
W. Stock   D   tp   1905–30s   (taken over by Hartkopf)
Stormer   1 : 32 'C' scale   shells
Strauss   US   tp   (later Louis Marx; *see also* Strauss Man)
Strauss Man   US   tp   (successor to Strauss; later Louis Marx)
Streamlux   AUS   dc   1950s–77?   (became Fun-Ho)
Strombecker   US   1 : 24   p kit and slot   (parent company of Tootsietoy)
Structo   US   steel construction toy, tp, cast iron   1917–
Sturditoy   US   steel
Sturdy   SA   (Chad Valley)
Summer Metal   HK
Sun   US   Rubber
Sunnyside   HK
Superchampion   (*see* Champion)
Supermaquatraction   H0   slot
Super Mini   TAI   tp friction   1980s
Superscale   GB   wm kit
Supershells   slot kits   (taken over by S.R.M.)
Surber   1 : 43
Sutherland Castings   GB   1 : 76/86   (buses, etc.; assoc. Cotswold)
S.V.P.-Peraboni   I   1 : 43/35   dc   1938

Taiyo   JAP   tp   1959   (incl. battery operated)
Talsalda   HK   1 : 32   p
Tamara   US
Tamiya   JAP   1 : 24   slot kits;   1 : 20/25/35/55   military
T.A.T.   HK
Taylor & Barrett   GB   dc   (*see also* F.G.T., T & B, F. G. Taylor, and Barrett

& Sons)
Taylormade 1 : 32 slot kits
T. Co. Dn (monogram of Tipp & Co., Nuremberg)
T.C.R. R/C
Technofix Dn (trademark of Gebrüder Einfalt, Nuremberg)
Tekno DK 1 : 43 dc
Tenaviv GR
Tester US p kits
Thameshead GB 1 : 60 wm kit
Timpo GB dc
Tin's Metal Mfy Ltd HK
Tin Wizard D cast kit
Tipp Dn tp 1912–71 (Ullmann family who formed Mettoy in UK 1934–;
trademark T.Co. and Tippco)
Tippco Dn (trademark of Tipp & Co., Nuremberg)
Titan GB slot shells
T.K. tp 1930s
T.N. JAP tp 1923– (Nomura Toys)
Toby Toys GB (involved with D.C.M.T. and Johillco)
Togi I 1 : 23 metal kit or made up
Tokyo Plamo 1 : 24/32 slot shells
Toman GB 1 : 76 wm kit
Tomica JAP 1 : 60/43 and all other scales dc (Tomy; incl. Dandy)
Tomte NL rubber
Tonka steel post-war
Tootsietoy US cast metal, dc from 1932 (prev. Dowst; *see* Strombecker)
Toycraft AUS wooden and p 1940s
Toy Founders US promo models
Toymaster JAP tp post-war
Toyopet
Toys of Yesteryear GB (*see* Hodges)
T.P.S. JAP tp 1956– (Toplay-T.P.S. Ltd)
Trailways US 1 : 43 p
Train Tronics US 1 : 87 p (with working electric lights)
Transport Replicas GB 1 : 86 wm kit (Varney; 1 : 43 briefly)
Tri-ang GB steel, wood, tp, p (*see* Lines Bros)
Trix Dn/GB tp (Stephan Bing, Oppenheimer and Erlanger took over Förtner
and Haffner 1927; construction kits taken over by Gama 1971)
Troger D 1 : 87 wm kit
Tron I 1 : 43 wm
Trucks of the World
Tsusho JAP (*see* Asahi and A.T.C.)
T.T. JAP tp
Tuckerbox AUS dc 1950s
Tudor Rose GB 1 : 10 polythene
Tuftots 1 : 118 (a Lone Star range)
Tula
Turner US tp friction drive 1920s/30s
Twinn-K H0 gauge slot
Tyco US 1 : 40 p

Ubilda (construction kits by Chad Valley)
U.D. HK dc

Uebelacker Dn tp 1871 (and again in 1934)
Ulrich US 1 : 87 wm kit (trucks)
Unis F tp
United JAP
Universal JAP
U.P.C. 1 : 32 p

Varney GB (*see* Transport Replicas)
V.B. F tp (*see* Victor Bonnet et Cie, Paris)
V de C GB 1 : 43 (made by L. M., and J. Day)
V.E.B. DDR tp 1947– (Volksligener Betrieb Mechanishe Spielwaren; formerly Brandenberg Lehmann factory)
Vébé F tp (*see* Victor Bonnet et Cie, Paris)
Ventura I 1947 (made at Progamiol)
Veritas NL 1 : 16 card
Verneurl
Veteran and Vintage GB wm (Dinky replicas)
Viceroy CA p
Victory US glass candy containers 1930s
Victory (*see* V.I.P.)
Vieux Tacots 1 : 32
Vilmer DK 1 : 50, etc.
Vindex US cast iron 1920s/30s
Vinil Line 1 : 43
V.I.P. 1 : 18/32 p (battery powered)
V.M.F. DDR 1 : 45
Volvo 1 : 30 promo
V.S.S. DDR 1 : 18/17 p

Wagner JAP 1 : 14 pewter and p
Walldorf D wm/p
Wallwork GB cast iron
W & T GB 1 : 76 wm kit
Wang Tin Ind. HK
W.D. HK p
Web DDR
Weeden (early traction engine)
Weekin (name for Chad Valley)
Wells GB tp 1919–32 (later Wells-Brimtoy)
Wells-Brimtoy GB tp 1932–*c.*1960
Wessex wm (pseudo-Dinky)
Western Models GB 1 : 43/76 metal kit or made up
Weston US 1 : 86 metal kit (later Campbell)
Weston R/C
Westward GB 1 : 76 wm kit (commercials)
Wheelworks US 1 : 86 metal kit
Whitanco (trademark of Whiteley Tansley)
Whiteley Tansley & Co. GB tp 1916–*c.*1929 (*see also* Whitanco)
Wiking D 1 : 40/90/160 p (made aircraft recognition models for Luftwaffe)
Wilkins US cast iron 1888–1919 (later Kingsbury tp/clockwork)
Willesco steam
A. C. Williams US cast iron 1920s/30s
Wills Finecast GB 1 : 24/43 (also Auto-Kits)

Wilson GB 1 : 72/43 wood/card/composition/p/kits 1934–50s (commercials)
Wimmer Dn tp 1928– (*see also* H.W.N.)
Gerald Wingrove GB Master Modeller
Winna AUS dc or bakelite 1940s/50s
Winross US 1 : 64/87 dc 1963– (commercials/promos; mainly based on White Freightliner)
Wizard GB (*see* Scorpio)
W.K. Dn tp (trademark of Wilhelm Krauss, Nuremberg)
Wolverine Supply Co. US tp 1930s ('Sandy Andy' tank, etc.)
Wonder 1 : 24/32 slot shells
Wonderland 1 : 24/32 slot shells (conn. Wonder?)
Woolbro p
W.R. Dn (trademark of William Rissmann, Nuremberg)
W Toys HK
Wyandotte US tp 1920s/40s

X-acto
X-EL Products US (reissued Joltan promos at first)
X.V.M. F polyester and wm 1975

Y JAP tp post-war
H. Yamada JAP tp 1914 (Günthermann copy with Lehmann trademark!)
Yanoman 1 : 16 metal
Yaxon I (took over from Forma)
Yesteryear, Models of GB (*see* Lesney)
Y.M. JAP tp
Yonezawa JAP (parent company of Diapet)

Zax I 1 : 43/75 dc 1938–47 on (made Bergamo)
Zebra GB dc (made by Benbros; *see also* Qualitoys)
Zechin JAP (assoc. with Grip)
Zee Toys US/HK 1 : 53, etc. dc
Zenke DDR
Ziss (*see* R.W.)
Zwicky CH
Zylmex HK 1 : 76, etc.

TIN-PLATE TOY MANUFACTURERS' TRADEMARKS

An alphabetical listing of trademarks of the more often encountered tin-plate toymakers. Included are details of founding (or principal) personalities where known, countries of origin, approximate dates of commencement and (where applicable) cessation of manufacture, and descriptions of the trademarks themselves where necessary.

Richard & Carl Adam: Königsburg, East Prussia *c.*1895–*c.*1905
(Figure standing on a globe)

Alps Shoji Ltd: Tokyo, Japan 1948–
(Mountain peaks)

Arnold: Nuremberg 1906–
Karl Arnold died 1946; then son-in-law Christian Ernst took over

Asahi Toy Co. Ltd: Tokyo, Japan 1950–
(Father Christmas carrying a sack)

Bandai: Tokyo, Japan 1950–

Bassett-Lowke Ltd: Northampton, England 1899– Wenman J. Bassett-Lowke died 1953
1968 Bassett-Lowke (Railways) Ltd
(Various, including two incorporating locos and signal)

 **Biller:** Nuremberg 1937– Hans Biller (ex-Bing)
(A clockwork key and 'B')

  **Gebrüder Bing:** Nuremberg 1863
Ignaz and Adolph Bing. Wholesalers
Manufacturers from 1879–1933
Ignaz Bing died 1919, then Stephan Bing
Receivership 1932. Karl Bub takeover 1933
(Very early – a female figure carrying a shield; at
the last – incorporating Karl Bub)

 **Blomer & Schüler:** Nuremberg 1919–74
(An elephant with howdah)

  **Victor Bonnet et Cie:** Paris, France 1912–c.50s
Took over Fernand Martin 1912

 **Brandstätter:** Germany 1876–
Andreas Brandstätter
Now Horst and Michael Branstätter
(Geobra)

 **Brimtoy:** London, England c.1914–32
Amalgamated with Wells 1932
(Nelson's column)

 **William Britain:** England c.1900–

 **KBN** **Karl Bub:** Nuremberg 1851–1966
Took over Carette designs 1917
KB Took over Bing designs 1933
Taken over by Frank Tarr (USA) 1967
(Early – a windmill; finally – incorporating Bing-
Werke)

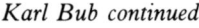

Karl Bub continued

Burnett Ltd: Birmingham (then London),
England *c*.1910–
Moved to London 1914
Later taken over by Chad Valley
(St George and dragon)

Cardini: Omegna, Italy 1922–28
(A winged arrow in a circle)

Georges Carette: Nuremberg 1886–1917
Georges Carette (died 1920s)
Ceased production 1917 (Bub took over some
designs)
(Early – a female figure surmounted by an angel;
latterly – a clockwork cogwheel)

Jouets André Citroën: Briare, France 1923–36
André Citroën
Sold to C.I.J. in 1936
(Citroën chevron appeared on radiator of each toy
vehicle)

Johann Distler: Nuremberg 1900–62
Johann Distler died 1923
Then Braun and Meyer till 1935/6
Then taken over by Ernst Volk
(Initially – a thistle; latterly – a globe)

Doll et Cie: Nuremberg 1898–1938*Peter Doll
and J. Sondheim, then *c*.1912 Max Beim
Joined in 1927 by Reichel (ex-Bing)
*Taken over by Fleischmann 1938 but name
retained

158

Hans Eberl: Nuremberg *c*.1900–29
Hans Eberl
Then (1902) Ludwig and Emil Schwartzbauer
Liquidated 1929
(A clown-like figure with legs astride and arms
akimbo within a circle)

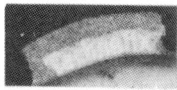

Gebrüder Einfalt: Nuremberg 1922–
Georg and Johann Einfalt
Now Alfred and Johann Einfalt
(Black triangle in white circle in black square –
Technofix)

Essdee: Germany 1920s
Little known, but toys appear made by Distler
(Boy running carrying box marked Essdee)

Faivre: France 1860–*c*.1918
Edmond Faivre, then E. F. Levevre
(The letters 'F' 'V' in a double box)

Falk: Germany 1897–1935
Joseph Falk
Took over Schönner designs 1910
Taken over by Ernst Plank 1935
(A lighthouse)

Georg Fischer: Nuremberg 1903–58
Georg Fischer
(A stylised 'GF' monogram)

H. Fischer & Co.:   Nuremberg *c*.1908–31/2
H. Fischer
Bankrupt in 1931/2
(A figure in armour or a fish)

J. Fleischmann: Nuremberg 1887–
Jean Fleischmann died 1917
Wife Käthe and brother continued
Took over Georg Staudt 1928
Took over some Doll designs 1938
Johann and Earl Fleischmann from 1940
(The letters 'GFN' in a black triangle, later a
script)

159

Förtner und Haffner: Nuremberg *c*.1920–27
Andreas Förtner and Johann Haffner
Taken over by Stephan Bing 1927 and name
changed to Trix (The word 'Anfoe' in a triangle)

G & K or Gundka: Brandenberg *c*.1920–*c*.1944
Originally Messrs Greppert & Kelch
Then Herr Hille

S. Günthermann: Nuremberg 1877–1965
S. Günthermann; then Adolf Weigel
Then Leonhard Günthermann from 1919
Taken over by Siemens 1965
(Initially – a male figure carrying a lance and
shield)

Gutmann: Paris, France post-war 1950s
Mery Gutmann
(A clown's face and the trade name MEMO)

Haji: Tokyo, Japan 1951–
Mansei Toy Co. Ltd

Hausser: Ludwigsburg, Germany (1936
Neustadt) 1904–
Otto and Max Hausser
(A stylised 'H' in the shape of a house, also the
trade name Elastolin)

Heller & Schiller: Oberslentensdorf,
Sudetenland (now Czechoslovakia) *c*.1930–45
(The name HUSCH in a circle)

Hess: Nuremberg 1826–1934
Mattheus Hess
Then Johann Hess from 1866

Höfler: Fürth 1938–54
Johann Höfler
Taken over by Ernst Bettag 1954
(A leaf containing the initials 'JH')

 **I.N.G.A.P. (Industria Nazionale Giocattoli Automatici Padova):** Italy 1919–72
Giovanni Casale   Giorgio Zattla   Pietro Zinelli   Tullio and Anselmo Anselmi
Then Mario Benacchio (died 1936)
Taken over by Eurotoys 1972
(Double-headed eagle bearing the initials)

  **Issmayer:** Nuremberg 1861–1933/4
Johann Andr. Issmayer (died 1922)
J. Weissberger (son-in-law) (died 1926)
 August Weissberger (son)
(Winged wheel)

  **J.E.P. (Les Jouets de Paris):** Paris, France 1928–65
(Previously S.I.F. from 1899; originally La Société Industrielle de Ferblanterie)

 **Jouef:** France c.1919–

 **Joustra:** Strasbourg-Neudorf 1934–
Guillaume Marx (ex-Bing)
(A lighthouse)

 **Keim:** Nuremberg c.1930s–60
Keim & Co.
Took over Josef Kraus and Wilhelm Krauss 1937/8

  **Kellermann:** Nuremberg 1910–
Georg Kellermann (died 1931)
Willy Kellermann from 1924 (son)
Then Helmuth Kellermann (son) from 1960

H. Kienberger: Nuremberg 1910–
Hubert Kienberger (died 1938)
Georg Levy (left 1916 to form own business)
Irmgard Kienberger (daughter) from 1938
Now grandson of founder
(An alarm clock with trade name KiCo, also
trade name Huki)

Kindler & Briel: Böblingen 1865–
Wilhelm Kindler
Then sons Willy and Paul Kindler
(A Father Christmas above the letters 'KBB', also
trade name Kibri)

Kingsbury: USA 1919–45
Harry T. Kingsbury
Took over Wilkins Toy Co. 1895
Name changed to Kingsbury 1919
*c.*1930 sons Chester and Edward Kingsbury took
over
Machine tools only from 1945

Köhler: Germany 1932–
Georg Köhler
(The letters 'G' and 'K' superimposed on a letter
'N', all in a triangle)

Kraus: Nuremberg 1910–39
Josef Kraus (left firm 1933)
Trade name Fandor from mother Fanny and aunt
Dora. Taken over by Keim & Co. 1937

Krauss: Nuremberg 1895–1938
Wilhelm Krau*ss* (note spelling)
Taken over by Keim & Co. 1937

Lehmann: Brandenberg (Nuremberg from 1951)
1881–
Ernst Paul Lehmann (died 1934)
Johann Richter from 1911 (cousin), took over 1934
Brandenberg factory (East Germany) became V.E.B.
(A bookbinder's press with monogram)

Georg Levy: Nuremberg 1920/21–71
Georg Levy (ex-Kienberger) left company 1934
Then Karl Ochs and name changed to
Nurnberger
Blechspielwarenfabrikation

Lineol: Brandenberg 1934–45
Oskar Wiederholz
(Three running ducks in line)

Lines Bros: London (then Merston and others), England 1919–80s
Walter, Arthur and William Lines (sons of owner of G. & J. Lines)
Took over Toy Store, Regent Street, 1931
Took over Meccano Ltd 1964 (incl. Dinky Toys and Hornby)
(An 'L' in a triangle, also trade names Tri-ang, Tri-angtois and Minic)

Lionel: New York (then Irvington, New Jersey), USA 1901–
Joshua Lionel Cowan (died 1965)
Taken over by Model Product Corpn (General Mills) 1970
(A lion standing on its hind legs within an 'L')

Mangold: Fürth 1882–
Georg Adam Mangold
Hans Mangold (son) from 1920
Made some Schuco toys under licence
Took over Trix in 1971
(Trade name GAMA from c.1924)

Markes: Ludenscheid 1904
Carl Markes
(A swallow in a circle with the trade name Dux)

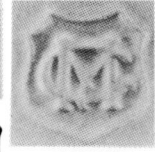

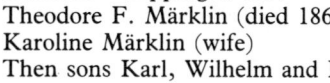

Märklin: Göppingen 1859–
Theodore F. Märklin (died 1866)
Karoline Märklin (wife)
Then sons Karl, Wilhelm and Eugen (who retired in 1935)
Joined by Emil Fiz 1892 and later Richard Safft
Eugen's son Fritz (from 1923) took over 1935, died 1961
(Various, including a stylised 'M' in the shape of a loco)

F. Martin: Paris, France 1878–1912
Fernand Martin (died 1919)
Taken over by Bonnet et Cie 1912

163

 **Marx:** New York, USA (and Dudley, England 1932) 1920–
Louis Marx
Took over Strauss Man & Co. 1920 (and many others)
Opened British branch in 1932
British branch now part of Dunbee-Combex Group
(The letters 'MAR' superimposed on a large 'X' in a circle)

  **Meccano (orig. Frank Hornby and Elliott & Hornby from 1901):**
Liverpool, England 1908–80s
Frank Hornby (died 1936)
(incl. Hornby boats and trains and Dinky Toys)
Taken over by Lines Bros 1964
(Various, but includes a bi-plane with Meccano on the wings and a red seal)

  **J. Ph. Meier:** Nuremberg 1879–c.1930
Johann Philipp Meier (died 1911)
Then Jean Weinberger
(A dog pulling a cart)

 **Mettoy:** Northampton; England 1934–
Philipp Ullmann (ex-Tipp & Co.)
(Also trade name Corgi for die-cast toys)

 **Moschkowitz:** Nuremberg (and England 1929) 1919–71
Max Moschkowitz

 M.T. (Modern Toys): Tokyo, Japan 1924–
K. K. Masotoku Toy Factory

 **Müller & Kadeder:** Nuremberg c.1900–c.1912
(A hot-air balloon)

Orobr: Brandenberg *c*.1910–22
Oro-Werke Reil, Blechschmidt and Müller

  **Paya:** Ibi, near Alicante (and later Alicante),
Spain 1906–
Hermanos Paya
(Various, including the word 'Paya' stylised as a
loco)

 Plank: Nuremberg 1866–*c*.1930s
Ernst Plank
Taken over by Schaller Bros
(A winged wheel surmounted by three stars,
above the initials 'E.P.')

 Rabbit: Tokyo, Japan 1950–
Usagiya

 **Rico:** Ibi, near Alicante, Spain 1920–
Santiago Rico Molina
Agapito Bernando Verdu
Jaime Esteve Bastand
(A bi-plane above the trade name 'R.S.A.')

 **Rissmann:** Nuremberg 1907–
Took over Martin Ettinger

 **Roitel:** France 1880–*c*.1920
Charles Roitel

Rossignol: Paris, France 1868–1962
Charles Rossignol

 **Schönner:** Nuremberg and Muggendorf
1875–1910
Jean Schönner
Then (1904) Adolf Dihlmann
Some designs taken over by Falk 1910
(A star and a winged wheel and initials 'J.S.' in a
lozenge)

Schreyer & Co.: Nuremberg 1912–
Heinrich Müller (died 1958) and partner Schreyer
(who later departed)
Then from 1958 Werner Müller (son) and
Alexander Girz
(Trade name Schuco; also (early) a clown holding
his legs behind the knees)

Fabrik-Marke

Schuhmann: Germany 1925–39
Adolf Schuhmann

Seidel: Nuremberg 1881–
Michael Seidel
Georg Seidel (son) from 1908
Gerhard Hamann (brother-in-law) from 1939
(A mountain goat on its hind legs on a
mountainside)

S.H.: Tokyo, Japan 1959–
Horikawa Toys

Staudt: Germany 1840/50–1928
Georg Leonhard Staudt
Heinrich Staudt (son) from 1887
Taken over by Fleischmann in 1928
(A view of a town)

Stock: Solingen 1905–*c.*1935
Walter Stock
Taken over by Paul Hartkopf 1930s
(Two crossed walking sticks in a circle)

Taiyo: Tokyo, Japan 1959–
Taiyo Koyzo Co. Ltd
(A stylised walking robot)

MADE IN JAPAN

Tipp: Nuremberg 1912–71
Miss Tipp Philip Ullmann from 1919–33
Ernst Horn (ex-Bing) 1935–45
Philip Ullmann regained control 1945
Henry Ullmann (son)

T.N.: Tokyo, Japan 1956–
Nomura Toys Ltd

T.P.S.: Tokyo, Japan 1950–
Toplay (T.P.S.) Ltd
(A hand with the small finger curving to touch
the thumb)

Trix: Nuremberg 1935–71*
Stephan Bing (ex-Bing), Oppenheimer and
Erlanger
Took over Andreas Förtner and Joh. Haffner
1927
Name changed to Trix 1935
Taken over by Ernst Volk 1938
*Taken over by Mangold (Gama) 1971

Uebelacker: Nuremberg 1871–?(1934)
Leonhard Uebelacker
Christian Uebelacker listed 1934. Maybe no
connection
(A figure of Neptune with trident being drawn
through the waves in a chariot by two sea-horses)

V.E.B. (Volkseigener Betrieb Mechanische,
Spielwaren): Brandenberg 1947–
Successors to Lehmann
Johann Richter to 1947

Wells: Islington (then Walthamstow), England
1919–50s
A. W. Wells
Took over Brimtoy Ltd 1932
Factory at Holyhead 1945–*c.*1959
Taken over by C. M. T. Wells Kelo Ltd *c.*1959
(Two brick-built traditional 'wishing' wells)

Whitanco: Liverpool, England 1916–*c.*1930
Whiteley, Tansley & Co. Ltd
(A spoked wheel bearing the trade name
Whitanco around its rim)

Wimmer: Nuremberg 1928–
Heinrich Wimmer (died 1970)
Ernst Wimmer (son) from 1950
(A scroll incorporating two 'smiley' faces and the
initials 'HWN')

167

INDEX

171